EYEWITNESS
INSECT

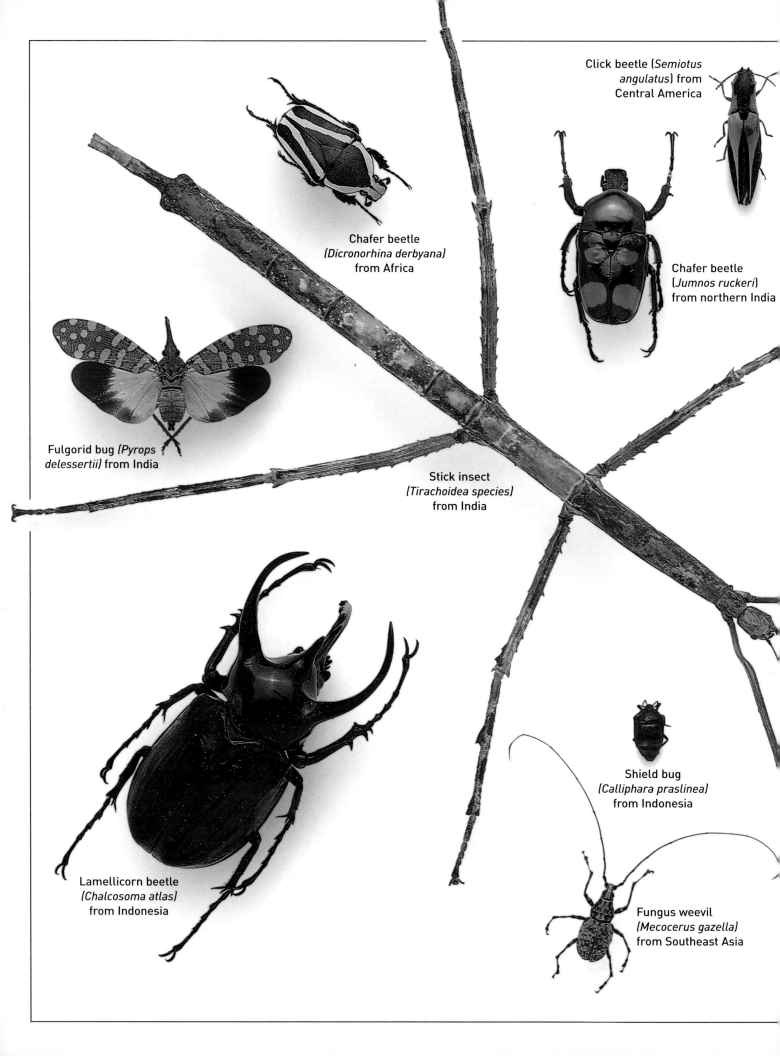

Click beetle (*Semiotus angulatus*) from Central America

Chafer beetle (*Dicronorhina derbyana*) from Africa

Chafer beetle (*Jumnos ruckeri*) from northern India

Fulgorid bug (*Pyrops delessertii*) from India

Stick insect (*Tirachoidea species*) from India

Shield bug (*Calliphara praslinea*) from Indonesia

Lamellicorn beetle (*Chalcosoma atlas*) from Indonesia

Fungus weevil (*Mecocerus gazella*) from Southeast Asia

Blowfly (*Calliphora vomitoria*) found worldwide

Tawny mining bee (*Andrena fulva*) from Europe

EYEWITNESS
INSECT

Written by
LAURENCE MOUND

Stag beetle (*Phalacrognathus muelleri*) from northern Australia

Bog bush cricket (*Metrioptera brachyptera*) from Europe

Leaf beetle (*Doryphorella 22-punctata*) from South America

Tortoise beetle (*Eugenysa regalis*) from South America

Shield bug (*Sphaerocoris annulus*) from Africa

Cuckoo wasp (*Stilbum splendidum*) from Australia

Longhorn beetle (*Callipogon senex*) from Central America

Rove beetle (*Emus hirtus*) from Great Britain

Shield bug (*Cantao ocellatus*) from Indonesia

Leaf beetle (*Doryphorella princeps*) from South America

Butterfly
(*Ancyluris formosissima*) from South America

Shield bug (*Poecilocoris latus*) from India

Bilberry bumblebee (*Bombus monticola*) from Europe

Dung beetle (*Phanaeus demon*) from Central America

Dung beetle (*Coprophanaeus lancifer*) from South America

Ropalidia wasp nest

Tree wasp (*Dolichovespula sylvestris*) from Europe

Longhorn beetle (*Sternotomis bohemanni*) from east Africa

Jewel beetle (*Chrysochroa chinensis*) from India

Tiger beetle (*Manticora scabra*) from east Africa

Giant ant (*Dinoponera grandis*) from Brazil

Chafer beetle (*Agestrata luzonica*) from the Philippines

Dusky sallow moth (*Eremobia ochroleuca*) from Europe

Chafer beetle (*Trichaulax macleayi*) from northern Australia

DK | Penguin Random House

Project editor Helen Parker   **Art editor** Peter Bailey
Senior editor Sophie Mitchell   **Senior art editor** Julia Harris
Editorial director Sue Unstead   **Art director** Anne-Marie Bulat
Special photography Colin Keates, Neil Fletcher, Frank Greenaway, Harold Taylor, Jane Burton, Kim Taylor, and Oxford Scientific Films

THIRD EDITION
Editor Sue Nicholson   **Managing editor** Camilla Hallinan
Managing art editor Martin Wilson   **Publishing manager** Sunita Gahir
Category publisher Andrea Pinnington   **Production editors** Andy Hilliard, Laragh Kedwell, Hitesh Patel   **Production controller** Angela Graef

RELAUNCH EDITION

DK DELHI
Project Editor Priyanka Kharbanda   **Project Art Editor** Neha Sharma
Assistant Editor Antara Raghavan   **Assistant Art Editor** Priyanka Bansal
DTP Designer Pawan Kumar   **Senior DTP Designer** Harish Aggarwal
Picture Researcher Sakshi Saluja   **Jacket Designer** Juhi Sheth
Managing Editor Kingshuk Ghoshal   **Managing Art Editor** Govind Mittal

DK LONDON
Senior Art Editor Spencer Holbrook   **Editor** Anna Streiffert Limerick
US Senior Editor Margaret Parrish   **US Editor** Jill Hamilton
Jacket Editor Claire Gell   **Jacket Design Development Manager** Sophia MTT
Producer, pre-production Gillian Reid   **Producer** Gary Batchelor
Managing Editor Francesca Baines   **Managing Art Editor** Philip Letsu
Publisher Andrew Macintyre   **Associate Publishing Director** Liz Wheeler
Art Director Karen Self   **Design Director** Philip Ormerod
Publishing Director Jonathan Metcalf

This Eyewitness ® Guide has been conceived by
Dorling Kindersley Limited and Editions Gallimard

First American Edition, 1990
This edition published in the United States in 2017 by
DK Publishing, 345 Hudson Street, New York, New York 10014

Copyright © 1990, 2003, 2007, 2017 Dorling Kindersley Limited
DK, a Division of Penguin Random House LLC
17 18 19 20 21   10 9 8 7 6 5 4 3 2
002—305102—June/2017

Published in Great Britain by Dorling Kindersley Limited

A catalog record for this book is available from the Library of Congress.
ISBN 978-1-4654-6248-0 (Paperback)
ISBN 978-1-4654-6253-4 (ALB)

DK books are available at special discounts when purchased in bulk for sales promotions, premiums, fund-raising, or educational use. For details, contact: DK Publishing Special Markets, 345 Hudson Street, New York, New York 10014 SpecialSales@dk.com

Printed and bound in China

A WORLD OF IDEAS:
SEE ALL THERE IS TO KNOW

www.dk.com

Contents

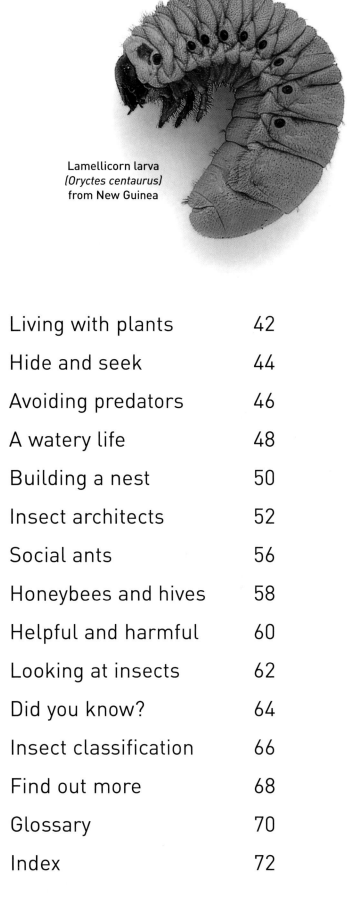

Lamellicorn larva
(Oryctes centaurus)
from New Guinea

The parts of an insect

Once an insect has reached adult size, it never grows any larger. This is because its entire body is covered by a hard external skeleton made of a horny substance called chitin. Young insects shed, or molt, this "exoskeleton" several times during their lives. The insect takes in extra air to make itself larger and splits the old skin, which falls off to reveal the new skeleton beneath.

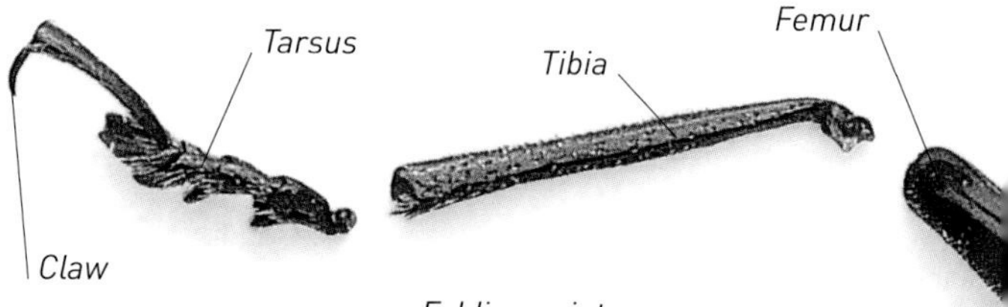

Tarsus

Claw

Tibia

Femur

Folding point

Front, or leading edge of wing

Tip, or apex, of wing

Base of wing folds underneath

Hind wing folded
In order to fit beneath the wing cases, the hind wings must be folded. The wing tip folds back at a special break called the folding point. The base of the wing is also folded underneath.

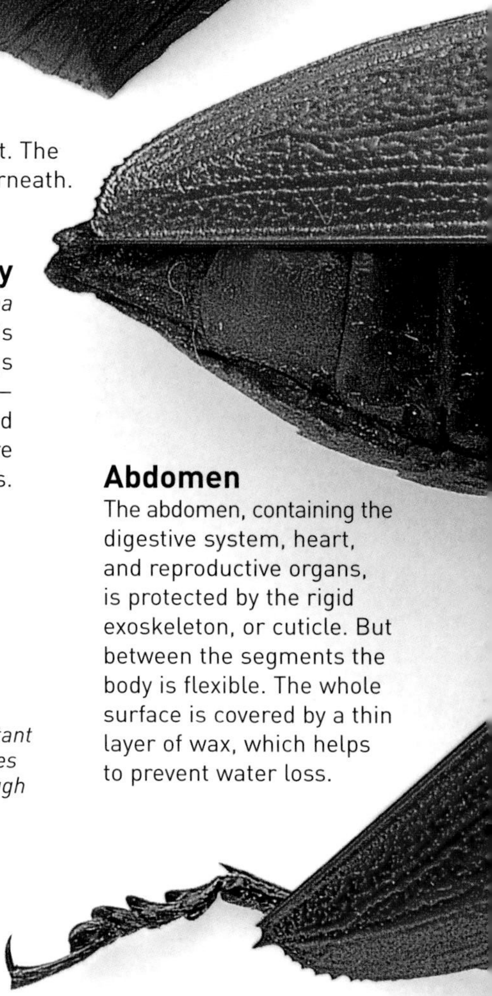

Beetle body
This jewel beetle (*Euchroma gigantea*) from South America is a typical insect with jointed legs and three distinct body regions— the head, thorax (chest), and abdomen. These regions are made up of ringlike segments.

Abdomen
The abdomen, containing the digestive system, heart, and reproductive organs, is protected by the rigid exoskeleton, or cuticle. But between the segments the body is flexible. The whole surface is covered by a thin layer of wax, which helps to prevent water loss.

Ganglion in head (brain)

Nervous system

Compound eye

Foregut breaks up food

Air sacs are important in supplying muscles in thorax with enough air for flight

Midgut digests food

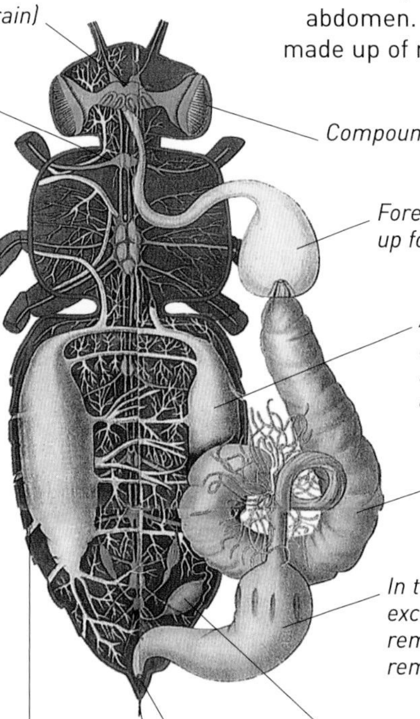

Internal anatomy
This diagram shows the internal anatomy of a worker bee. The digestive system (yellow) is a long tube divided into the foregut, midgut, and hindgut. The breathing, or respiratory, system (white) contains a network of tubes, through which air passes from the spiracles to every part of the body. In the abdomen are two large air sacs that supply the flight muscles in the thorax with air. The simple nervous system (blue) is formed by one main nerve, which has knots of nerve cells, or ganglia, along its length. The ganglion in the head is the bee's brain. The store of poison that leads to the bee's sting is shown in green.

In the hindgut, excess water is removed from the remains of food.

Air enters breathing tubes through spiracles

Food waste is ejected through anus

Poison store for sting

Sting

Front wings
In beetles, the front pair of wings is adapted as a pair of hard wing cases called elytra. These protect the body and are often brightly colored.

Legs

Insects have three pairs of jointed legs made up of four main parts: the coxa joins the leg to the thorax; the femur (thigh) is the most muscular section of the leg; the tibia (lower leg) often carries spines for self-defense; and the tarsus (foot) has two claws that often contain a small pad for gripping onto smooth surfaces.

Armor plating

A tank (right) is like a large beetle, with its hard outer skin protecting the important inner workings from being damaged by enemies.

Tarsus has between one and five segments

Tibia

Femur

Coxa

Second and third segments of the thorax

Coxa

Each foot bears two claws for climbing on rough surfaces.

Feeding in information

The head houses the brain and important sense organs such as the eyes, the antennae, and the palps (feelers), which give the insect information about the taste and smell of its food.

Antennae

Antennae can be long and thin, as in crickets, or short and hairlike, as in some flies. But whatever their shape, they bear many sensory structures that are able to detect smells and air movements.

Compound eye

Compound eyes

"Compound" eyes consist of hundreds of tiny, simple eyes, which can detect movement in almost every direction at once.

First segment of thorax bears front legs

Thorax

The thorax is made up of three segments. The first bears the first pair of legs, while the second and third segments each bear a pair of wings and a pair of legs.

Segmented antenna detects vibrations and smells

Spiracle

Claw

Leading edge of hind wing

Hind wing outstretched

As the wing cases are lifted, muscles inside the thorax pull on the leading edge of the hind wings, making them open.

Wing case, or elytron

A spiracle can be closed to prevent the entry of air

A breath of fresh air

Insects breathe air through a network of tubes (tracheae) that extend into the body from pairs of openings in the cuticle called spiracles.

What is an insect?

Ground beetle

Ladybug beetle

Beetles
Beetles belong to the order Coleoptera. They have tough front wings (elytra) that fold over the hind wings and body like a protective case.

Insects are the most successful creatures in the animal kingdom. They are found in all types of habitats, both on land and in water. Their size means they can fit into very small places and need little food to live. Insects are arthropods, which are a type of invertebrate (animal without a backbone). They have a hard, protective exoskeleton and jointed legs. However, insects are different from other arthropods because they have only six legs. Each species is a member of a larger group, or order, made up of other insects with the same physical features.

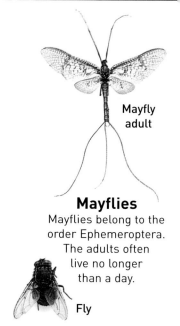

Mayfly adult

Mayflies
Mayflies belong to the order Ephemeroptera. The adults often live no longer than a day.

Fly

Flies
Flies belong to the order called Diptera, meaning "two wings," because, unlike other insects, flies have only one pair of wings.

Wasp

Front wings are larger than hind wings

Bee

Ant

Wasps, ants, and bees
These insects belong to the order Hymenoptera and have two pairs of thin, veined wings. Many females in this group are armed with a sting.

Cockroaches
Adult cockroaches have hardened front wings that overlap each other. Young cockroaches are wingless.

Dragonfly

Dragonflies and damselflies
These closely related insects belong to the order Odonata. Their large jaws are specially adapted to catch flies.

Earwig

Earwigs
Earwigs belong to the order Dermaptera. Their hind wings are folded under their very short front wings.

Piercing, sucking mouthparts

Wings hard at base, soft at tip

Bug

Stick insect

Bugs
True bugs belong to the order Hemiptera, which means "half wing." The front wings of many larger bugs have hard bases with soft tips.

Grasshopper

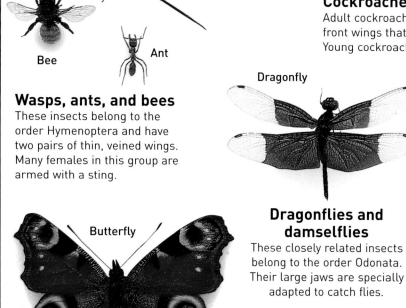

Butterfly

Butterflies and moths
Butterflies and moths belong to the order Lepidoptera. The tiny scales on their wings give them their beautiful colors.

Moth

Crickets and grasshoppers
These insects have strong hind legs used for jumping and singing. They belong to the order Orthoptera.

Stick insects
When resting, these insects look just like the leaves and twigs they eat.

Not insects

Many people confuse other arthropods with insects. Spiders and scorpions have four pairs of legs, rather than three, as in insects, but their head and thorax are fused together. Unlike insects, they have no wings and no antennae. Crabs, shrimp, wood lice, and centipedes all have many more jointed legs than insects. In contrast, an earthworm has no legs at all. Slugs, snails, and starfish have a very different structure that is not based on segments.

Pedipalps are specially adapted to form pincers

Scorpion

Scorpions
Scorpions, like spiders, have eight legs. They catch their prey with specially adapted limbs called pedipalps.

Shrimp

Shrimp
These sea creatures have 10 jointed legs—eight for walking and two for feeding and defense.

Vertebrates
This monkey is a vertebrate, meaning it has a backbone. Vertebrates breathe with lungs or gills. None of them has six legs, and their bodies are not divided into segments.

Millipede

Head

Ringlike segments

Earthworms
All earthworms are made up of many ringlike segments. Unlike insects, they have no legs and no hard parts.

Earthworm

Each segment bears four legs.

Wood louse

Wood lice
Wood lice, or pill bugs, live in cool, damp places, under stones and logs. When danger threatens, they roll into a tight, round ball of scaly armor.

Beach fleas
These strange creatures look like insects, but they have 10 legs, rather than six. They live in damp sand on beaches all over the world.

Millipedes
It is easy to see a millipede's head because, like insects, it has a pair of antennae. Its body is divided into many segments, each of which bears two pairs of legs.

Antenna

Centipedes
Unlike millipedes, centipedes have only one pair of legs on each segment. They capture their prey with their "poison claws," a specially adapted front pair of legs with fangs. Large species can give a painful bite.

Pedipalps used as feelers

"Poison claws"— modified front legs— are used to catch prey

Chelicerae (jaws)

Leg

Spiders
This tarantula from Sri Lanka is one of the world's largest spiders. The leglike pedipalps next to the head are used as feelers. The large jaws inject poison into their prey and, as in all spiders, the food is sucked into the body as a liquid.

Centipede

Tarantula

The first insects

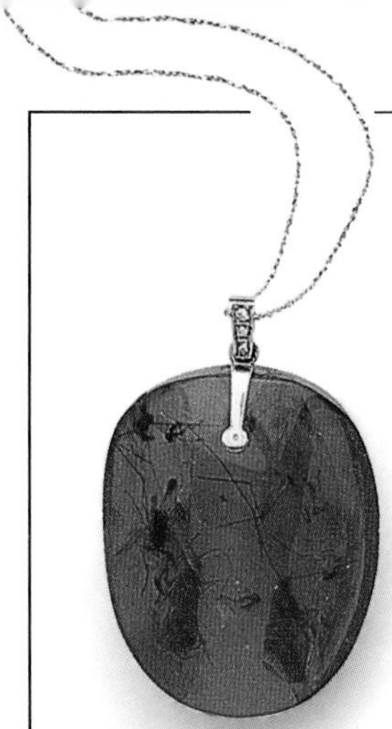

The first winged insects appeared on Earth more than 300 million years ago. Early fossils show that a few of these insects, such as dragonflies and cockroaches, would have looked very similar to present-day species. But most of the oldest insect fossils represent groups that are no longer alive today. Some of these early insects were probably hindered by large, unfolding wings, with spans of up to 30 in (70 cm), that prevented them from making a quick escape, and made them sitting targets for hungry predators.

Insect jewelry
This piece of Baltic amber (above) contains three quite different types of flies.

Limestone fossil of a moth's wing from southern England

Show your colors
Pigments in the scales of this fossilized wing have altered the process of fossilization, so that parts of the pattern can still be seen.

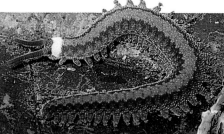

Living ancestors?
This peripatus has a soft body like a worm, but it has clawed legs like an insect and a similar breathing system.

Springtails
Springtails live in damp places all over the world. This species, shown here on the underside of a limpet, lives on the shore. Once counted as a primitive insect, it is now classified separately.

Wing

Delicate legs

How amber is formed

Amber is the fossil resin of pine trees that grew over 40 million years ago. Insects attracted by the sweet scent became trapped on its sticky surface. In time, the resin, including the trapped insects, hardened and was buried in the soil. Millions of years later, it was then washed into the sea.

Modern-day "sweat bee" (*Trigona* species)

Early cranes
About 35 million years ago, this crane fly (above) became trapped in muddy sediment at the bottom of a lake or pond in the USA. The sediment was so fine that when it turned to stone, even details of the wings and legs were preserved. With its floppy legs and wings, this fossilized specimen looks very similar to modern crane flies.

Bee in copal
This magnified piece of copal (a type of resin) shows a beautifully preserved "sweat bee." The bee looks very like the present-day specimen shown above.

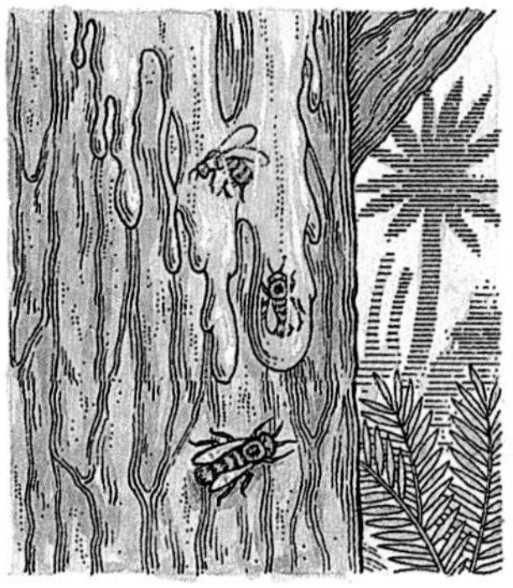

A sticky end
Crawling and flying insects become trapped for ever in the pine resin released by tree trunks.

Oldest dragonfly

This fossilized folded wing, found in England, belongs to the oldest-known dragonfly. The dragonfly flew 300 million years ago and had a total wing span of 8 in (20 cm), much larger than that of modern species.

Broken wing

Flowering plants

The arrival of flowering plants about 100 million years ago created a new source of food for insects, in the form of pollen and nectar. Insects thrived because of this new food, and the flowering plants thrived because of the variety of pollinating insects.

Largest dragonfly

This dragonfly (*Tetracanthagyna plagiata*) from Borneo (right) is a member of the largest dragonfly species still in existence, with a wingspan of 6 in (15 cm). The largest dragonfly ever known is a fossilized specimen from the USA, with a wing span of 24 in (60 cm).

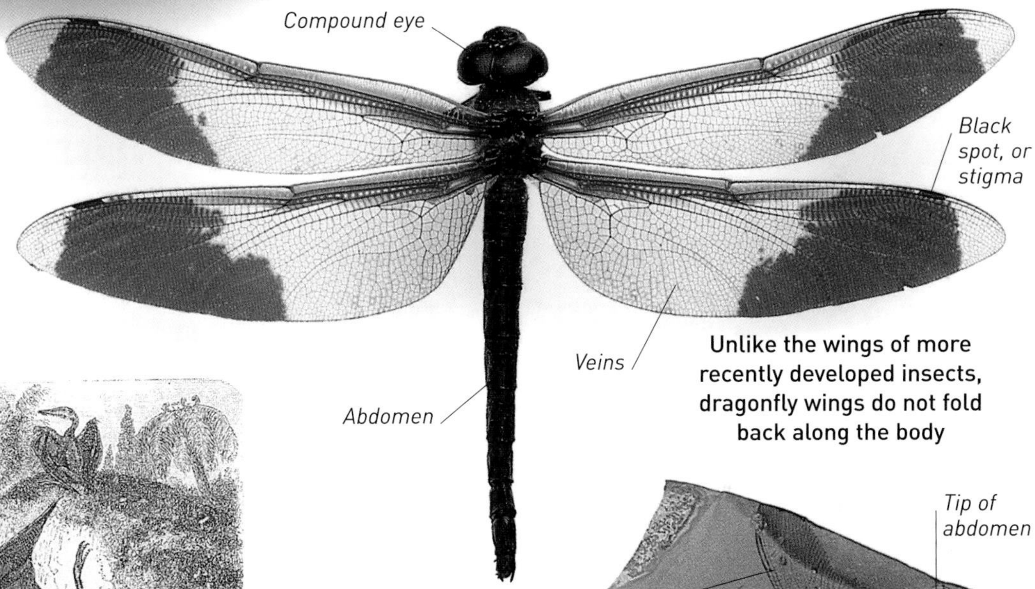

Compound eye

Black spot, or stigma

Veins

Abdomen

Unlike the wings of more recently developed insects, dragonfly wings do not fold back along the body

Tip of abdomen

Veins on wings

Dragonfly predators

The artist of this engraving (above) clearly had more imagination than biological knowledge. Fossils prove that early dragonflies were skilled fliers and would not have been so easily caught by a pterosaur.

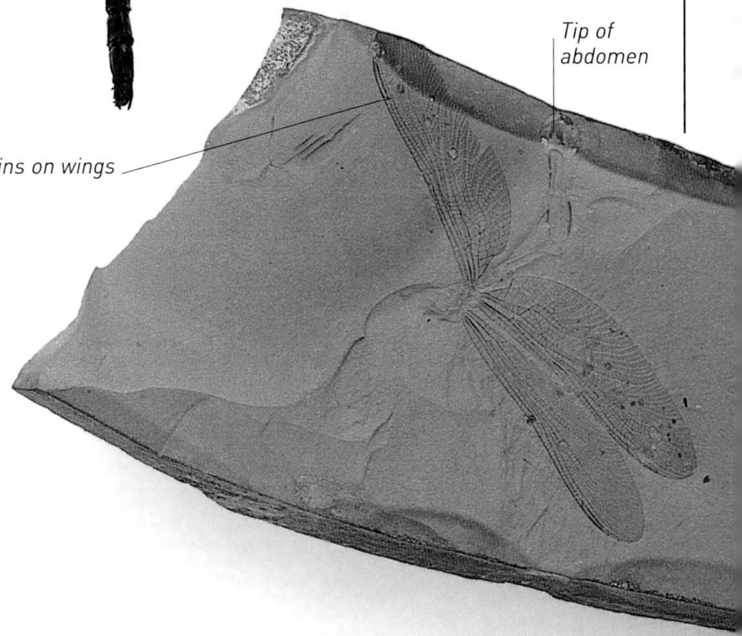

Drowned earwig

The lake deposits at Florissant, Colorado, are about 35 million years old. They contain many well-preserved insect fossils because of the fine sediment from which the rocks were formed.

Present-day earwig
(*Labidura riparia*)

Turned to stone

Even though this fossilized dragonfly appears to be missing a wing, the veins on the other wings can be seen quite clearly.

Crumpled wings
A newly emerged adult cicada has soft, crumpled wings. Blood pumps into the wings' veins making them expand. As the veins harden, the wings straighten, ready for flight.

Wings and flight

Insects were the first creatures to fly. Flight enabled them to search for food and to escape quickly from predators. Later, wings became important for attracting a mate—by being brightly colored, by producing a scent, or by making sounds. The first flying insects had two pairs of wings that did not fold. More recent insects, such as wasps, butterflies, and beetles, have developed various mechanisms for linking their front and hind wings to produce two, rather than four, flight surfaces that beat together. The true flies have lost one pair of wings altogether.

Fringed veins

Fringed wings
Small insects often have difficulty flying. The fringed veins on this magnified mosquito wing (above) probably act like the flaps on an airplane wing, helping to reduce "drag."

Cricket songs
Male crickets produce "songs" with their wings to attract mates. The base of the left front wing (above left) has a rigid file that is scraped against a drumlike area on the right front wing (above right).

Antenna

Eye

1 Before takeoff
Like any airplane, a large insect such as this cockchafer beetle (*Melolontha melolontha*) must warm up its engines before flying. Before taking to the air, beetles will often open and shut their wing cases several times to check that they are in good working order. It is not unusual to see moths rapidly vibrating their wings before takeoff to warm up their flight muscles.

Antenna spread to sense the air currents

Claws on feet enable beetle to grip plant firmly, ready for takeoff

Wing cases start to open

Hind wings folded beneath wing cases

2 Unfasten the wings
The hardened wing cases of the front wings are separated as the cockchafer prepares to take off from the top of the plant. The antennae are spread to check the air currents.

Wing cases, or elytra, protect the beetle's more delicate hind wings, which are folded up underneath.

Abdomen

Front margin of wing, or costa

Tip, or apex

Inner margin

Outer margin   *Vein*

Flash colors

Many insects that are perfectly camouflaged when at rest have brightly colored wings, which they flash when disturbed. As soon as the insect settles again, it seems to disappear, thus confusing a would-be predator. This grasshopper (*Ornithacris pictula magnifica*, left), probably uses its beautiful lilac wings for this purpose.

Scale

Color scales

The overlapping scales on butterfly wings are really flattened, ridged hairs that often form beautiful patterns.

Halteres help fly balance in the air

Balancing

Insects often have great difficulty balancing in gusty winds. Flies have overcome such problems by reducing one pair of wings to special knoblike balancing organs, called halteres; these are probably important for landing upside-down on ceilings.

Wing cases help give the beetle lift

Fully opened wings begin to beat

Hind legs outstretched may act as rudders in the air

4 We have lift-off

With a spring from the legs, the cockchafer rises upward. The hind wings provide the driving force, but the curve of the rigid front wings provides lift as the speed increases.

Wing cases spread wide to allow the wings to unfold

Joint in wing unfolds

Large hind wings unfold

Wing membrane

3 Reach for the sky

The wing cases are spread, and the thin membranous hind wings, which provide the driving force, automatically unfold as they are raised. In this vulnerable position, the beetle cannot afford to hesitate.

Segmented abdomen

Wing

Vertical muscle contracts, and wings move up

Thorax

Horizontal muscle contracts, and wings move down

Moving the wings

Most of the power for flapping the wings is provided by large horizontal and vertical muscles in the thorax. Other muscles at the base of the wings adjust the angle of each stroke and determine the direction of flight.

Through an insect's eyes

We do not know what sort of image insects have of the world. We know that a bee can see a person move several feet away—but does it just see a moving shape, or can it tell that the shape is a human? We also know that some bugs are attracted to ultraviolet light and the color yellow, but are not attracted to blue or red. But do they see colors, or shades of black and white? Dragonflies can catch mosquitoes in flight at dusk, when it is too dark for these small flies to be seen by humans—but does the dragonfly see them, or does it respond to their sound and movement? The subject of insect senses is full of such questions.

Three simple eyes, or ocelli, are sensitive to light

Light attraction

At night, bright lights attract many insects. Night-flying insects navigate by keeping the natural light of the moon at a constant angle to their eyes. An artificial light is treated in the same way; insects fly straight toward the light, but when they reach it, they circle around it continuously.

Natural light

Ultraviolet light

Ultraviolet light

These two brimstone butterflies have been photographed in natural light (left) and in ultraviolet light (right). Insects may not see a yellow butterfly with four orange spots, but a gray insect with two large dark gray areas. Many flowers rely on ultraviolet vision to attract pollinating bees; the bees are guided to the nectar by lines called honey guides, which are visible only in ultraviolet light.

Sense hairs all over the head give the wasp extra information about its surroundings.

The antennae detect odors and measure the size of the cells during nest building.

A waspish face

The head of a typical insect has a pair of large compound eyes as well as three simple eyes on top. The compound eyes of this wasp (*Vespula vulgaris*, above) extend low down on the cheeks toward the jaws, but are not developed on the part of the face where the antennae lie. The powerful jaws are used to cut up food, to dig with, and to lay down new nest material. The brilliant yellow and black pattern warns other animals that this insect has a dangerous sting.

Powerful jaws are the hands and tools of the wasp

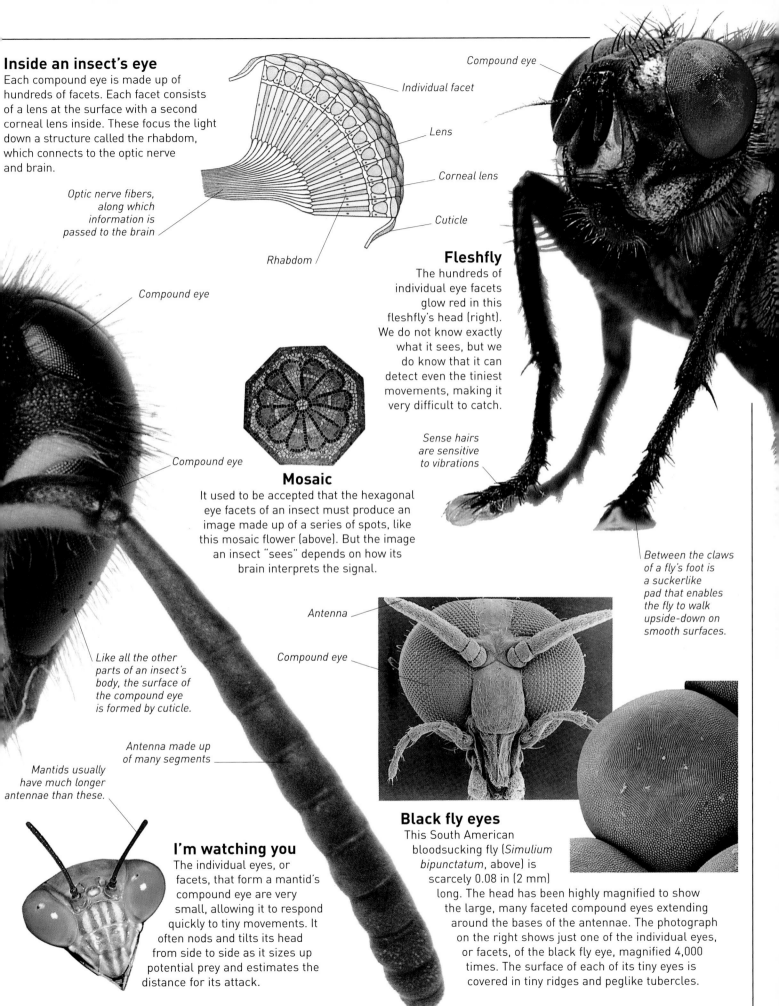

Inside an insect's eye

Each compound eye is made up of hundreds of facets. Each facet consists of a lens at the surface with a second corneal lens inside. These focus the light down a structure called the rhabdom, which connects to the optic nerve and brain.

Optic nerve fibers, along which information is passed to the brain

Individual facet

Lens

Corneal lens

Cuticle

Rhabdom

Compound eye

Fleshfly

The hundreds of individual eye facets glow red in this fleshfly's head (right). We do not know exactly what it sees, but we do know that it can detect even the tiniest movements, making it very difficult to catch.

Compound eye

Sense hairs are sensitive to vibrations

Compound eye

Mosaic

It used to be accepted that the hexagonal eye facets of an insect must produce an image made up of a series of spots, like this mosaic flower (above). But the image an insect "sees" depends on how its brain interprets the signal.

Between the claws of a fly's foot is a suckerlike pad that enables the fly to walk upside-down on smooth surfaces.

Like all the other parts of an insect's body, the surface of the compound eye is formed by cuticle.

Antenna

Compound eye

Antenna made up of many segments

Mantids usually have much longer antennae than these.

I'm watching you

The individual eyes, or facets, that form a mantid's compound eye are very small, allowing it to respond quickly to tiny movements. It often nods and tilts its head from side to side as it sizes up potential prey and estimates the distance for its attack.

Black fly eyes

This South American bloodsucking fly (*Simulium bipunctatum*, above) is scarcely 0.08 in (2 mm) long. The head has been highly magnified to show the large, many faceted compound eyes extending around the bases of the antennae. The photograph on the right shows just one of the individual eyes, or facets, of the black fly eye, magnified 4,000 times. The surface of each of its tiny eyes is covered in tiny ridges and peglike tubercles.

Touch, smell, and hearing

Feeler
This featherlike structure is the antenna of a male moth. The many side branches are covered in tiny sensory hairs.

For many insects, the world is probably a pattern of smells and tastes. Alarm chemicals are produced by many insects, so that the other members of a colony can respond quickly. Ants lay down a chemical trail and constantly touch each other to pass on their nest odor. Female moths produce chemicals capable of attracting males from great distances. This insect world of smells and tastes also includes vibrations and sounds undetected by humans. These vibrations may be detected by insects through well-formed "ears," as on the front legs of crickets and on the abdomen of grasshoppers, or they may be picked up through the legs and antennae.

Antenna

Simianellus cyaneicollis at about five times life-size

Antlers
Both male and female Indian beetles have remarkable antlerlike antennae, which are usually held back along the body with the branches closed.

Biting jaws

Weevil's head (*Cyrtotrachelus* species) at about seven times life-size

Rostrum used for drilling into plant seeds and stems

Clubbed tip is covered in sensory hairs

Elbowed antenna

Eye

Head swivels inside thorax

Nosy weevil
The biting jaws of a weevil are at the end of the long snout, or rostrum. The sensory hairs on the tips of the "elbowed" antennae are used to explore the surface the weevil is feeding on.

Each hair is ridged.

Ball and socket joint

Magnified hairs
These hairs (left) from around the mouth of a carpet beetle larva have been magnified 1,000 times. Each hair has its own "ball and socket" joint at the base and ridged sides. The hairs are probably used for detecting vibrations.

Butterfly antenna

Butterfly antenna, magnified 2,000 times

Antenna
The surface of this butterfly antenna is covered with tiny sensitive pegs, or tubercles, and there are thin areas of cuticle with minute scent-sensitive hairs.

Feeling fine

This cricket (right) was found in a cave in central Nigeria. It has the longest antennae for its body size ever seen. These "feelers" are probably used to detect vibrations and currents of air and may help the cricket to find its way in the dark.

Long palps for manipulating food in dark

Sensitive antennae help the cricket find its way in the dark

Pair of long "cerci" at tip of abdomen are covered in sensory hairs

Cave cricket (*Phaeophilacris* species), actual size

Underside of wing showing perfume brushes

Perfume brushes

This male South American forest butterfly (*Antirrhea philoctetes*) has a curious cluster of hairs on its front wing. These hairs brush against a patch of "scent scales" on its hind wing. The brush picks up the scent scales and scatters the scent to attract females.

Antenna fan blades

European chafer beetle (*Melolontha melolontha*) at about five times life-size

Eye

Chafer fans

All scarab beetles have fan-shaped antennae like this chafer. When the beetle is walking about, the fan blades are usually closed, but when the beetle starts to fly, they are fanned out to detect the direction of the wind and any smells it may be carrying.

Lateral branch of antenna

Eye

Antenna is divided into many segments

Longhorn beetle (*Cynopalus wallacei*) at about four times life-size

Longhorn antlers

Longhorn beetles are so-called because of their long antennae. The antennae of most species are simple and unbranched, or have a few small side branches. This male longhorn (above) from Malaysia has spectacular long side branches, each of which is covered in tiny sense hairs, making the antennae doubly sensitive.

Cricket's leg (*Oxyecous lesnei*) at about eight times life-size

Joint

Femur

Ear opening

Tibia

Ears on knees

The front legs of crickets and weta have a small swelling just below the knee. This is their "ear" and consists of a drumlike membrane, called a tympanum, on either side of the leg. This tympanum is extremely sensitive to sound vibrations.

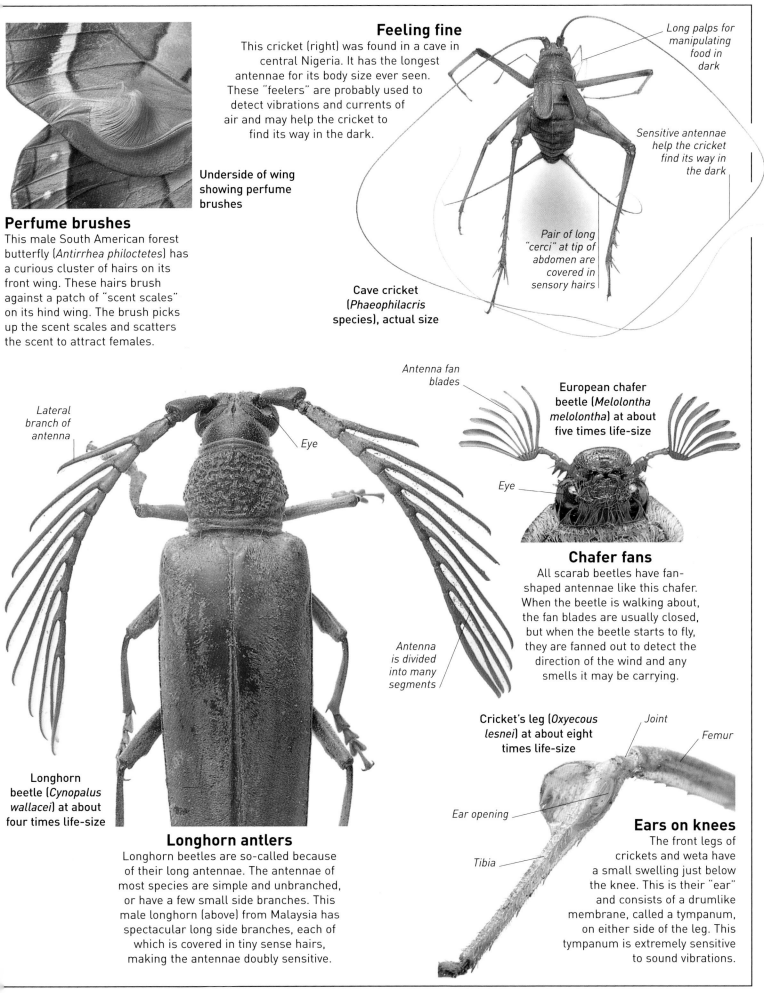

Legwork

Legs are important to most creatures for walking, running, and jumping, as well as for generally keeping the body off the ground. Insects have found even more uses for their legs. Bees have little brushes and baskets on their legs for collecting and storing pollen, and many insects' legs are modified for fighting or for holding on to the opposite sex when mating. Some water insects have flattened legs with long hairs that work like paddles or oars; others have long, delicate, stiltlike legs for walking on the surface without sinking.

Cleaning legs

Cleaning legs
Flies are covered in hairs, which must be cleaned regularly if the insect is to fly effectively. The feet of houseflies have special pads between the claws that enable the insect to walk upside-down on smooth surfaces.

Propellerlike feet can bury this cricket in seconds

Wings coiled like a spring

Going down
The propellerlike feet of this desert-dwelling cricket enable it to dig a hole in the sand and disappear in seconds. The ends of the wings are coiled to keep them out of the way.

Hind wings tilted above body

Front legs outstretched, ready for touchdown

Front wings curved to scoop up the air

1 Touching down
Landing safely is always a problem when flying. This locust has its legs spread wide, its hind wings tilted, and its front wings curved to catch the maximum amount of air. The wing shape of birds is adjusted in the same way when landing, to enable them to slow down and drop gently to the ground.

2 Preparing to jump
The locust gets ready to jump by bringing its hind legs into its body. The large muscles in the thigh (femur) are attached to the tip of the tibia (shinbone). When these muscles shorten, or contract, the leg straightens, throwing the insect into the air.

Bouncing boys
Unlike humans, who can jump, land, and jump again in one action, insects usually need to rest for a moment between jumps.

Mottled markings on wings help conceal insect on the ground

Tibia

Femur

Compound eye

Tibia

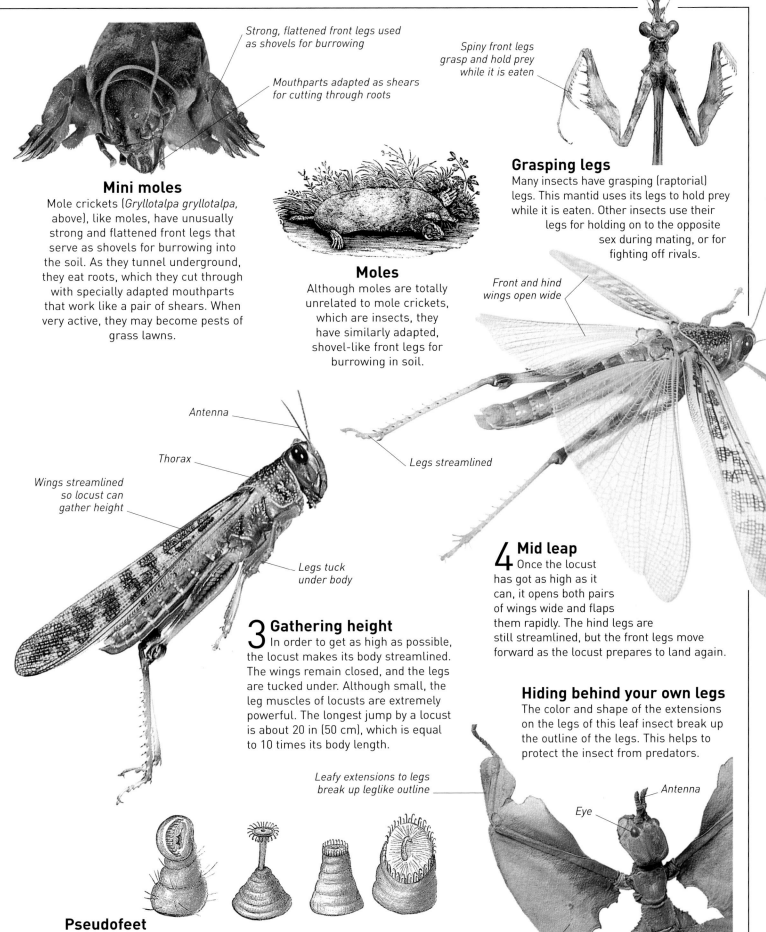

Strong, flattened front legs used as shovels for burrowing

Mouthparts adapted as shears for cutting through roots

Mini moles
Mole crickets (*Gryllotalpa gryllotalpa*, above), like moles, have unusually strong and flattened front legs that serve as shovels for burrowing into the soil. As they tunnel underground, they eat roots, which they cut through with specially adapted mouthparts that work like a pair of shears. When very active, they may become pests of grass lawns.

Moles
Although moles are totally unrelated to mole crickets, which are insects, they have similarly adapted, shovel-like front legs for burrowing in soil.

Spiny front legs grasp and hold prey while it is eaten

Grasping legs
Many insects have grasping (raptorial) legs. This mantid uses its legs to hold prey while it is eaten. Other insects use their legs for holding on to the opposite sex during mating, or for fighting off rivals.

Front and hind wings open wide

Antenna

Thorax

Wings streamlined so locust can gather height

Legs streamlined

Legs tuck under body

3 Gathering height
In order to get as high as possible, the locust makes its body streamlined. The wings remain closed, and the legs are tucked under. Although small, the leg muscles of locusts are extremely powerful. The longest jump by a locust is about 20 in (50 cm), which is equal to 10 times its body length.

4 Mid leap
Once the locust has got as high as it can, it opens both pairs of wings wide and flaps them rapidly. The hind legs are still streamlined, but the front legs move forward as the locust prepares to land again.

Hiding behind your own legs
The color and shape of the extensions on the legs of this leaf insect break up the outline of the legs. This helps to protect the insect from predators.

Leafy extensions to legs break up leglike outline

Antenna

Eye

Pseudofeet
The "legs" on the abdomen of caterpillars, known as prolegs, are actually muscular extensions of the body wall. Caterpillars use these prolegs for movement.

Greens and browns blend in with leafy surroundings

Mouthparts and feeding

Most insects have three pairs of jaws. The mandibles are used for chewing, while the maxillae help push food into the mouth. The third pair forms the lower lip (labium). In some insects, the jaws are modified into piercing needles, long sucking tubes, or absorbent sponges.

Bush cricket
This bush cricket is feeding on a flower. It holds the plant with its front legs, while the large and powerful sawlike mandibles chew it up.

Flea bites
This old engraving shows the flea's sucking tube surrounded by two pairs of palps, or sensory organs.

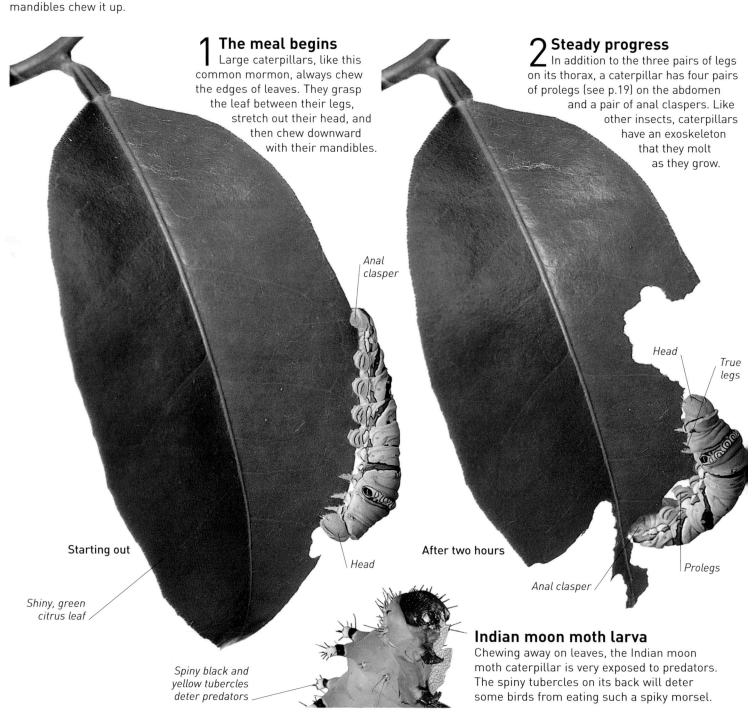

1 The meal begins
Large caterpillars, like this common mormon, always chew the edges of leaves. They grasp the leaf between their legs, stretch out their head, and then chew downward with their mandibles.

2 Steady progress
In addition to the three pairs of legs on its thorax, a caterpillar has four pairs of prolegs (see p.19) on the abdomen and a pair of anal claspers. Like other insects, caterpillars have an exoskeleton that they molt as they grow.

Anal clasper

Head

True legs

Starting out

Head

After two hours

Anal clasper

Prolegs

Shiny, green citrus leaf

Spiny black and yellow tubercles deter predators

Indian moon moth larva
Chewing away on leaves, the Indian moon moth caterpillar is very exposed to predators. The spiny tubercles on its back will deter some birds from eating such a spiky morsel.

Ants and aphids

Small plant-sucking bugs, such as aphids, are often protected by ants, who may even build a small shelter over the bugs. The ants feed on "honeydew," a sugary substance produced by the aphids that would otherwise build up and kill the aphid colony. One way to control aphid populations on trees is to stop the ants from climbing up and protecting them.

Piercing mouthparts

This tabanid fly has long mouthparts for drinking nectar from flowers. Many types of tabanid flies use their mouthparts to pierce the skin and suck up blood. They can feed on humans, but usually feed on the blood of monkeys. These flies are not delicate feeders like mosquitos and produce a very painful open wound.

Compound eye

Piercing, sucking mouthparts

After eight hours—on to the next leaf

3 Halfway there
The caterpillar works its way up and down the leaf.

After six hours

4 The end is in sight
Caterpillars usually feed at night to avoid predators.

Proleg

5 Dinner is over
After eight hours the leaf has gone, and the caterpillar is ready to look for the next one. A few more leaves like that and it will be ready for its final molt.

Head

Black and yellow markings ward off predators

Caterpillar breathes through spiracles on each segment

True legs on the thorax

When the jaws close, the teeth overlap to cut grubs in half.

After four hours

Compound eye

Spongelike labium for absorbing liquids

Compound eye

Butterfly head
This engraving shows how a butterfly's feeding tube (proboscis) coils up under the head. Adult butterflies do not have mandibles. The proboscis is made from the maxillae, each of which has become very long and pressed against the other.

Fly head
In houseflies and blowflies, the mandibles and maxillae are not developed. The spongelike structure used by these flies to pick up liquids is formed from the labium, which is simply the lower lip in other insects.

All cut up
The teeth on the jaws of this East African ground beetle overlap when the jaws close. This scissorlike action enables it to cut up grubs and even large beetles in the soil.

Battling beetles

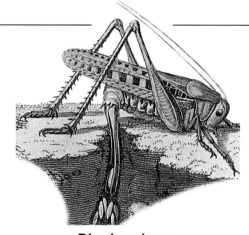

Some species of insect, such as grasshoppers and cockroaches, produce very large numbers of offspring, but limited supplies of plants to feed them, as well as hungry predators, help to limit insect populations. Some insects, such as those beetles that feed on dead wood, compete for both food and breeding sites. The males of many of these beetle species have large horns or jaws to fight off rivals.

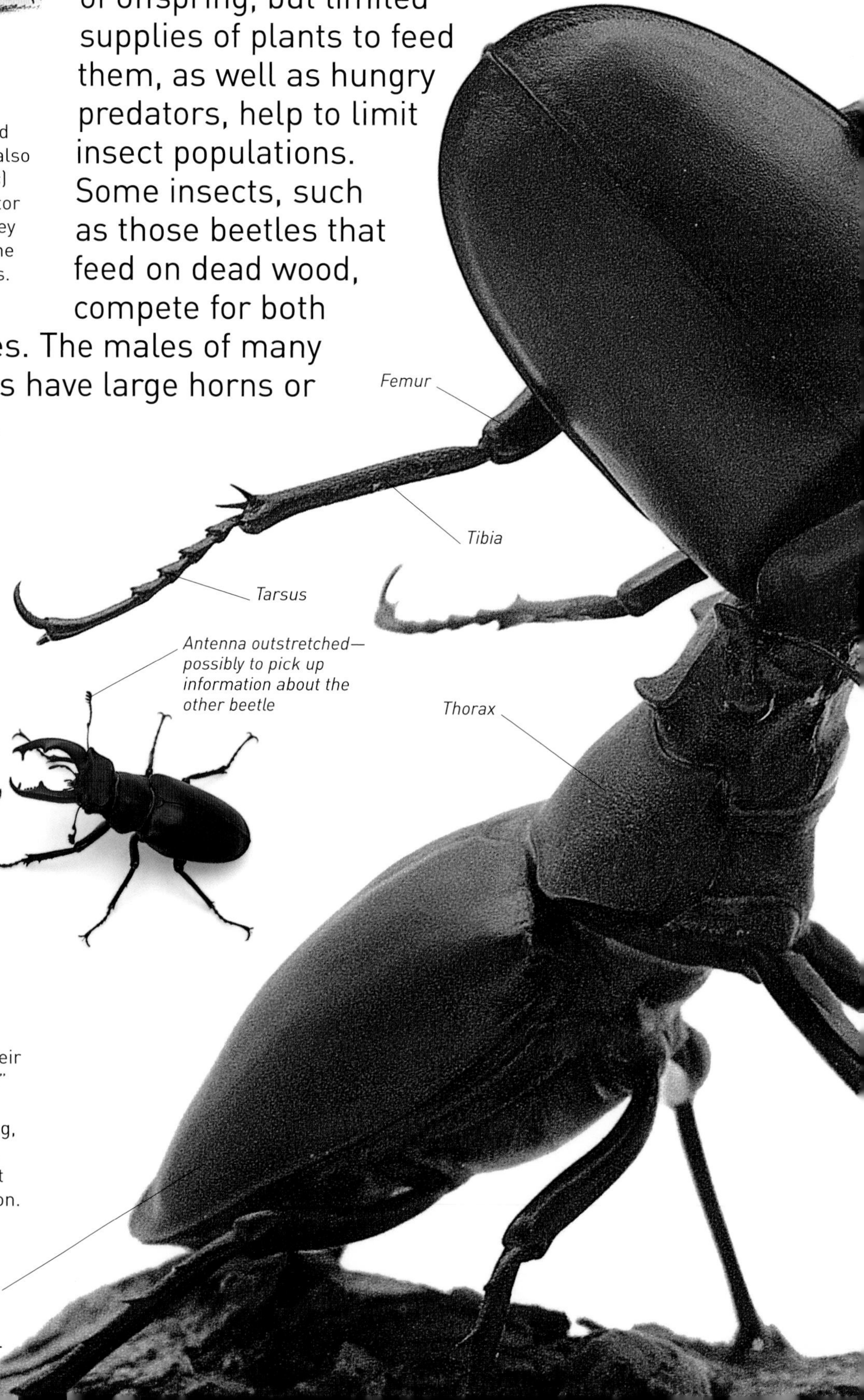

Digging deep

Grasshoppers lay their eggs around grass roots. In contrast, locusts and also this bush cricket (*Decticus albifrons*) drill into the soil with a long ovipositor and lay their eggs underground. They then fill in the hole and rake over the surface to conceal it from parasites.

Femur

Tibia

Tarsus

Antenna outstretched— possibly to pick up information about the other beetle

Thorax

Antlerlike jaws

Let's see who's boss around here!

1 Eyeing up the opposition
Stag beetles, like these two from Europe (*Lucanus cervus*, above), get their name from the large branched "horns" of the male. These are really greatly enlarged jaws that are used for fighting, much like a real stag uses his antlers. A male defends his territory, usually at dusk, by adopting a threatening position.

Hard, black, protective wing case

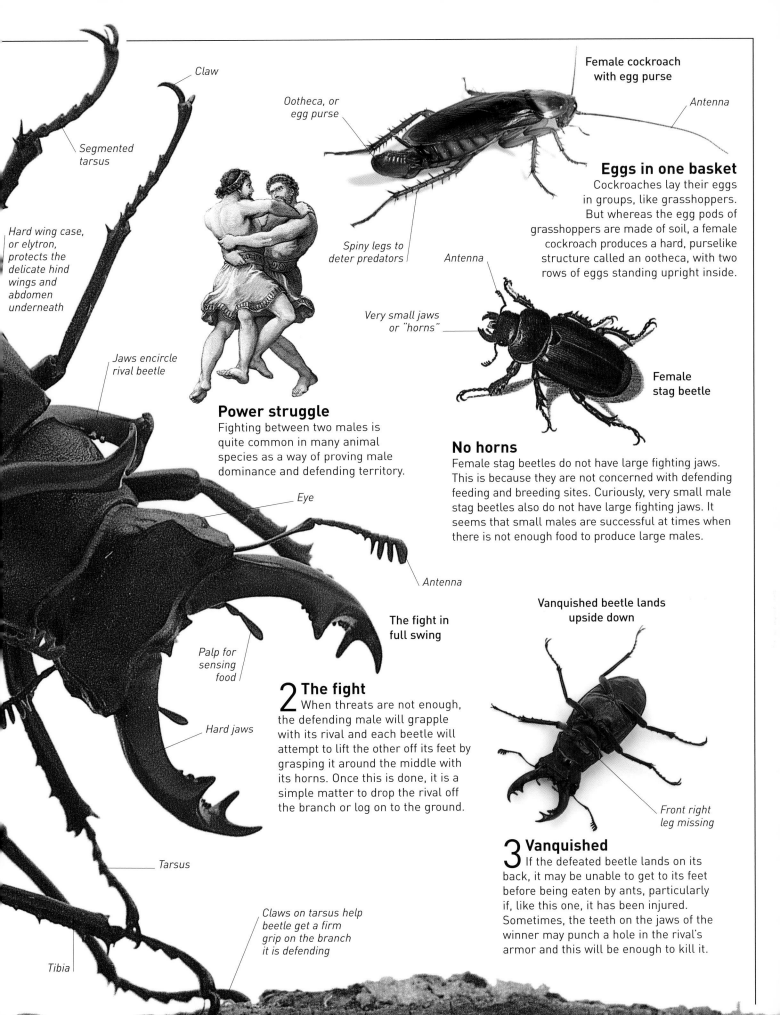

Claw

Segmented tarsus

Hard wing case, or elytron, protects the delicate hind wings and abdomen underneath

Jaws encircle rival beetle

Ootheca, or egg purse

Spiny legs to deter predators

Female cockroach with egg purse

Antenna

Eggs in one basket
Cockroaches lay their eggs in groups, like grasshoppers. But whereas the egg pods of grasshoppers are made of soil, a female cockroach produces a hard, purselike structure called an ootheca, with two rows of eggs standing upright inside.

Antenna

Very small jaws or "horns"

Female stag beetle

Power struggle
Fighting between two males is quite common in many animal species as a way of proving male dominance and defending territory.

No horns
Female stag beetles do not have large fighting jaws. This is because they are not concerned with defending feeding and breeding sites. Curiously, very small male stag beetles also do not have large fighting jaws. It seems that small males are successful at times when there is not enough food to produce large males.

Eye

Antenna

The fight in full swing

Palp for sensing food

Hard jaws

2 The fight
When threats are not enough, the defending male will grapple with its rival and each beetle will attempt to lift the other off its feet by grasping it around the middle with its horns. Once this is done, it is a simple matter to drop the rival off the branch or log on to the ground.

Vanquished beetle lands upside down

Front right leg missing

3 Vanquished
If the defeated beetle lands on its back, it may be unable to get to its feet before being eaten by ants, particularly if, like this one, it has been injured. Sometimes, the teeth on the jaws of the winner may punch a hole in the rival's armor and this will be enough to kill it.

Tarsus

Tibia

Claws on tarsus help beetle get a firm grip on the branch it is defending

Complete metamorphosis

Metamorphosis means "change of body form and appearance". The most advanced insects go through several stages of growth before turning into adults, in a process known as complete metamorphosis. The eggs hatch to produce larvae (caterpillars, grubs, or maggots) that are quite unlike adult insects. The larvae grow and molt several times, finally producing a pupa (chrysalis). Inside the pupa the whole body is reorganized, and a winged adult then emerges.

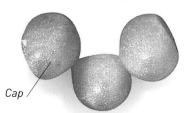

Larva emerges

Cap

Mating

Male and female Mexican bean beetles look very similar and mate frequently.

Eggs

Female Mexican bean beetles lay their eggs in large groups on the underside of leaves. Each egg stands on end and takes about a week to hatch.

1 Egg hatches

Pores at the top of the egg allow air to reach the larva inside. About a week after the egg has been laid, the cap at the top breaks and the larva emerges.

Old larval skin

New pupal skin

Old larval skin with long spines

New pupal skin with short spines

4 About to change

The larva attaches itself to the underside of a netted leaf, ready to pupate. The larval skin is shed, revealing soft, new pupal skin, which hardens quickly.

Larva feeding on plant shoot

Eating leaves

Mexican bean beetles feed on the fleshy parts of leaves both as larvae and adults.

Dead, lacy leaves on which larvae have fed

5 Resting

During the pupal stage all the muscles, nerves, and other structures dissolve, and new limbs, with new muscles and nerves, are formed. In the picture above, the adult beetle's yellow wing cases and the first segment of the thorax can be seen through the spiny skin of the pupa.

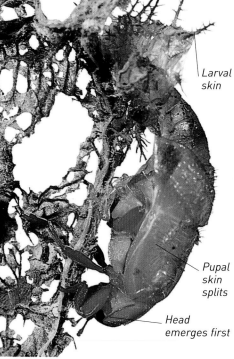

Larval skin

Pupal skin splits

Head emerges first

6 Ready to feed

The thin, spiny pupal skin splits along the underside, and the smooth young adult slowly emerges, head first.

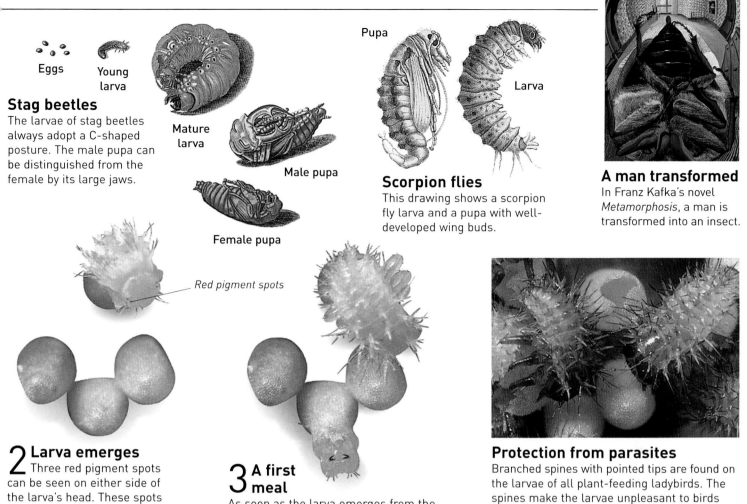

Stag beetles

The larvae of stag beetles always adopt a C-shaped posture. The male pupa can be distinguished from the female by its large jaws.

Eggs

Young larva

Mature larva

Male pupa

Female pupa

Pupa

Larva

Scorpion flies

This drawing shows a scorpion fly larva and a pupa with well-developed wing buds.

A man transformed

In Franz Kafka's novel *Metamorphosis*, a man is transformed into an insect.

Red pigment spots

2 Larva emerges

Three red pigment spots can be seen on either side of the larva's head. These spots are associated with simple eyes.

3 A first meal

As soon as the larva emerges from the egg, it turns around and eats the shell, which contains valuable nutrients.

Protection from parasites

Branched spines with pointed tips are found on the larvae of all plant-feeding ladybirds. The spines make the larvae unpleasant to birds and may deter parasites from laying eggs.

Old larval skin and pupal skin remains attached to leaf

7 No spots

The young beetle is yellow and has no spots, although the wing cases quickly harden. Before the beetle can fly, it needs to hold up its wing cases and expand its wings to allow them to dry. This process takes two to three hours.

Young adult

8 One more pest

After about 24 hours the adult spots appear on the wing cases, but the copper color takes about a week to develop fully. In 1918, the Mexican bean beetle was accidentally imported to the eastern United States and spread rapidly toward Canada. Today, it is a serious pest of bean crops in the USA.

From nymph to adult

Some insects, such as cockroaches, termites, and damselflies, go through a gradual transformation process known as incomplete metamorphosis. Their young, or nymphs, look like small versions of the adults. Very young nymphs have no wings, but older nymphs have "buds" on the thorax, inside which the adult wings develop. At each molt these wing buds get longer, until finally a nymph molts and an adult emerges.

Male

Tip of female's abdomen

Female

Lovehearts
During mating the male damselfly clasps the female's neck using the tip of his abdomen. The female then loops her abdomen forward in order to mate. They may fly together in this position for some time, often forming a heart shape with the male's head down at the tip and the female's head at the top of the heart.

Eye

Water flea being eaten by nymph

Mask

Nymph prey
Damselfly nymphs have a special lower jaw called a mask that shoots out to capture prey.

Young nymph
The time from egg to adult may take a few months or as long as three years depending on the species. Young nymphs are often transparent to help them hide from predators.

This young nymph has lost one of its gills—it should have three

Wing buds

Gills

Mature nymph

Mature nymph
When fully grown, a nymph often uses camouflage to enable it to hide both from its prey and from predatory fish. Its wing buds can be seen extending from the thorax over the first three segments of the abdomen.

Earwigs
Female earwigs sometimes dig a small hole in which to lay their eggs. They then stay with the eggs in order to protect them. Even when the young nymphs emerge, the female remains with them until they are ready to fend for themselves.

Gills
Dragonfly and damselfly nymphs absorb oxygen and get rid of carbon dioxide in the same way that fish do—by means of gills. But, unlike a fish, the gills of a damselfly nymph are not on the head, but in the form of three fan-shaped structures on the tail.

The mature nymph crawls out of the water so that the adult can emerge

The adult emerges

Although the damselfly nymph lives under water, whereas the adult flies, the mature nymph has a similar structure to the adult. It has the flight muscles and deep thorax, but the body and wings need to grow, and the nymphal mask must be shed. These changes are prepared within the nymph under water. Once in the air, it must change to an adult and fly quickly, usually in about two hours, or it will be eaten by some other animal.

Legs hold on tightly to the stem

As blood is pumped into the thorax, it begins to swell.

Wing buds

Abdomen

Tail gills have all been bitten off by a predator

1 Out of water

Above the water surface, the nymph digs its claws into the plant stem. The emerged adult will cling on for several hours until it is ready to fly. This nymph has lost all three gills to a predator. The wing buds are no longer pressed tightly against its abdomen, and blood is pumped into the thorax to make it swell.

Adult head starts to separate from the nymphal skin

Skin splits along back of thorax

Nymphal legs remain attached to the plant

2 The skin splits

The increased pressure of the blood in the thorax makes it expand very quickly, and suddenly, the skin splits along the back. The adult head is clear as it starts to separate from the nymphal skin.

Adult's front legs

Mask is left behind

Adult head

Wing is gently pulled out of wing-bud case

3 Breaking free

The adult head and thorax have now broken free from the nymphal skin. The front legs of the adult have also been withdrawn from the skin of the nymphal front legs. These remain firmly attached to the plant. The crumpled wings are gradually pulled from the wing-bud case.

Continued on next page

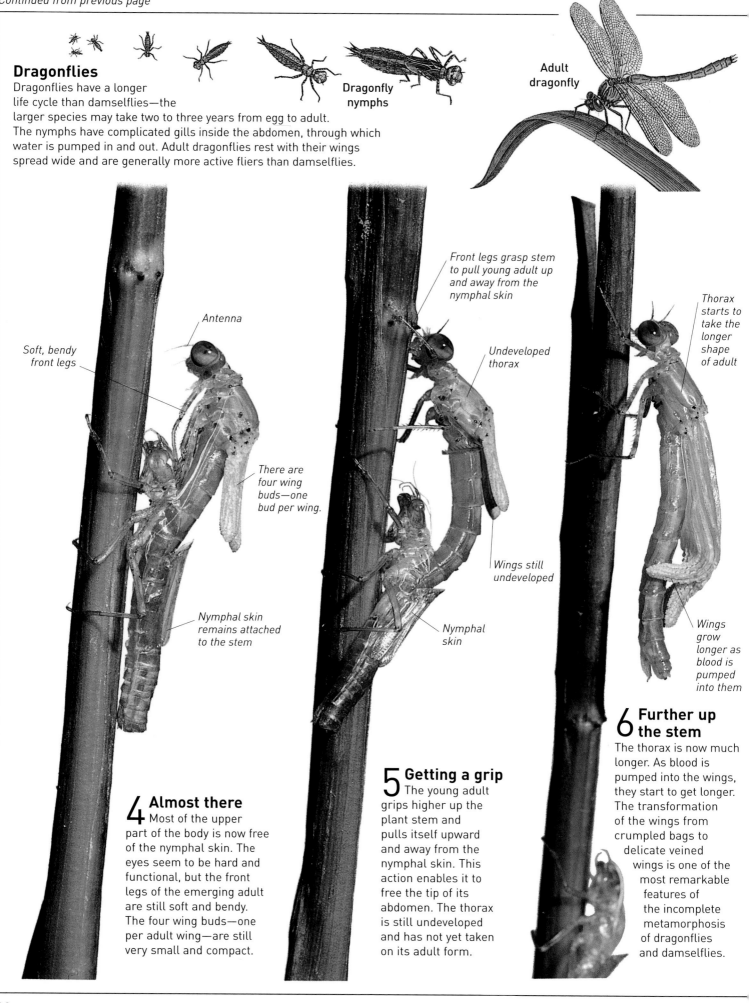

Dragonflies

Dragonflies have a longer life cycle than damselflies—the larger species may take two to three years from egg to adult. The nymphs have complicated gills inside the abdomen, through which water is pumped in and out. Adult dragonflies rest with their wings spread wide and are generally more active fliers than damselflies.

Dragonfly nymphs

Adult dragonfly

Antenna

Soft, bendy front legs

There are four wing buds—one bud per wing.

Nymphal skin remains attached to the stem

Front legs grasp stem to pull young adult up and away from the nymphal skin

Undeveloped thorax

Wings still undeveloped

Nymphal skin

Thorax starts to take the longer shape of adult

Wings grow longer as blood is pumped into them

4 Almost there

Most of the upper part of the body is now free of the nymphal skin. The eyes seem to be hard and functional, but the front legs of the emerging adult are still soft and bendy. The four wing buds—one per adult wing—are still very small and compact.

5 Getting a grip

The young adult grips higher up the plant stem and pulls itself upward and away from the nymphal skin. This action enables it to free the tip of its abdomen. The thorax is still undeveloped and has not yet taken on its adult form.

6 Further up the stem

The thorax is now much longer. As blood is pumped into the wings, they start to get longer. The transformation of the wings from crumpled bags to delicate veined wings is one of the most remarkable features of the incomplete metamorphosis of dragonflies and damselflies.

Damselflies

These delicate-looking insects are found near water. They have four similarly shaped, net-veined wings, which they hold above the body when resting. The damselfly shown here is a female of the species *Coenagrion puella*. The females of this species have a black back and brilliant green sides; the males have a blue back.

Close-up

This photograph shows the head of an adult male damselfly. It has large compound eyes and powerful chewing mouthparts. The legs are bunched behind the mouth for holding prey.

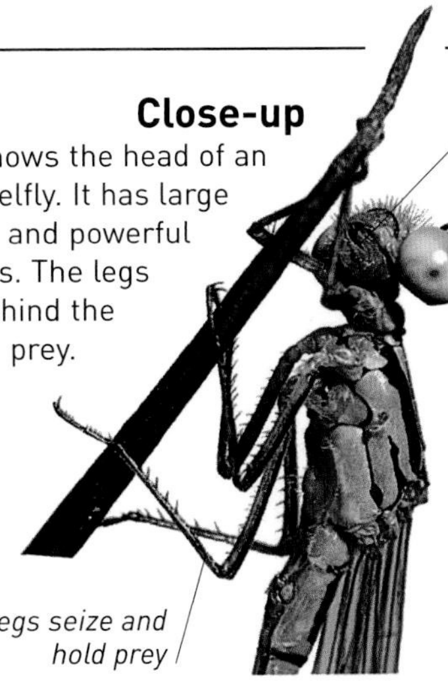

Strong, chewing mouthparts

Large compound eye for spotting prey

Legs seize and hold prey

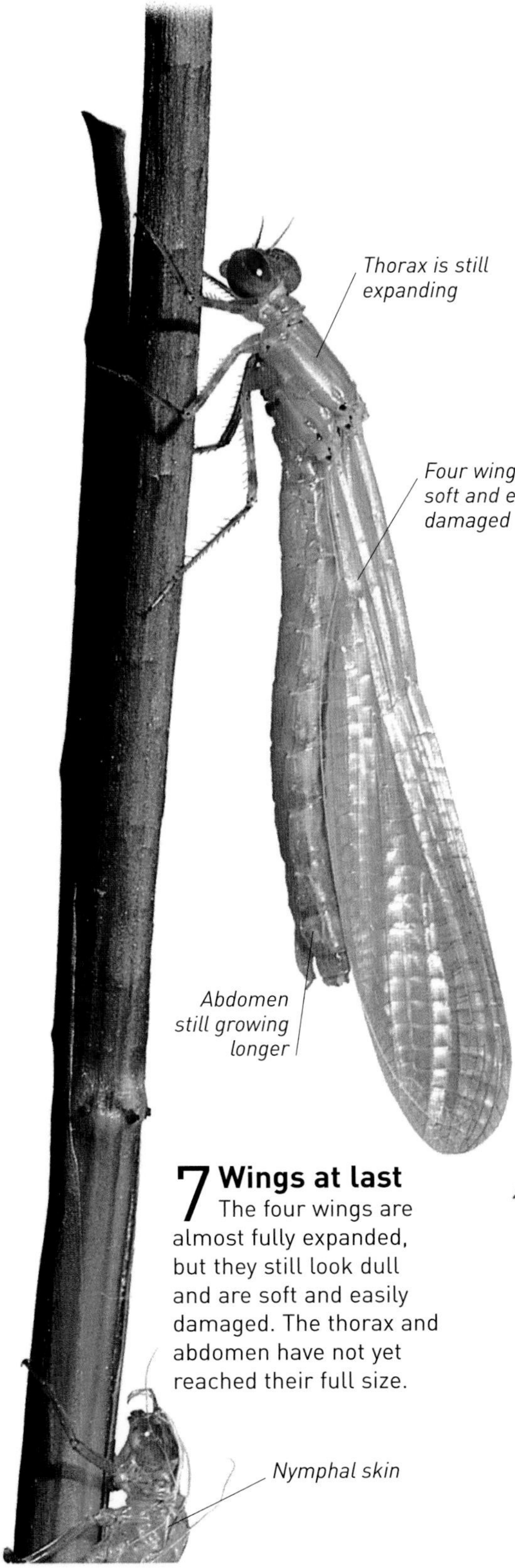

Thorax is still expanding

Four wings are soft and easily damaged

Abdomen still growing longer

7 Wings at last

The four wings are almost fully expanded, but they still look dull and are soft and easily damaged. The thorax and abdomen have not yet reached their full size.

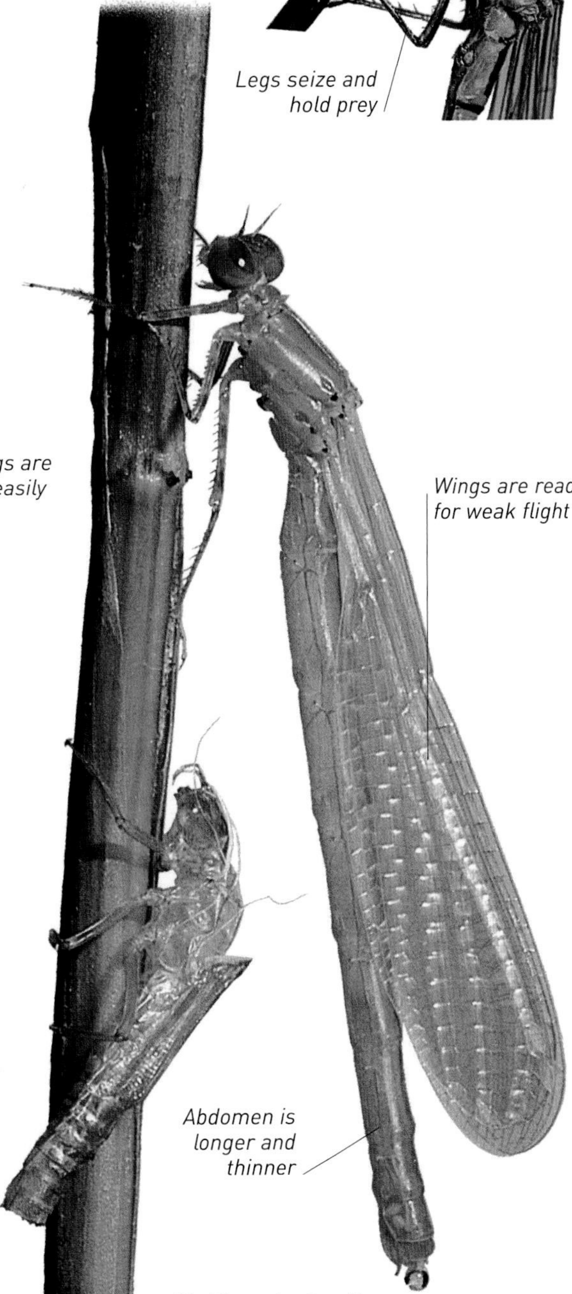

Nymphal skin

Wings are ready for weak flight

Abdomen is longer and thinner

8 Ready to fly

When the abdomen reaches its full length, the damselfly is ready to fly weakly, although the wings still look milky. The colors remain yellowish for many hours, and it will be several days before she gets her typical black and green color pattern.

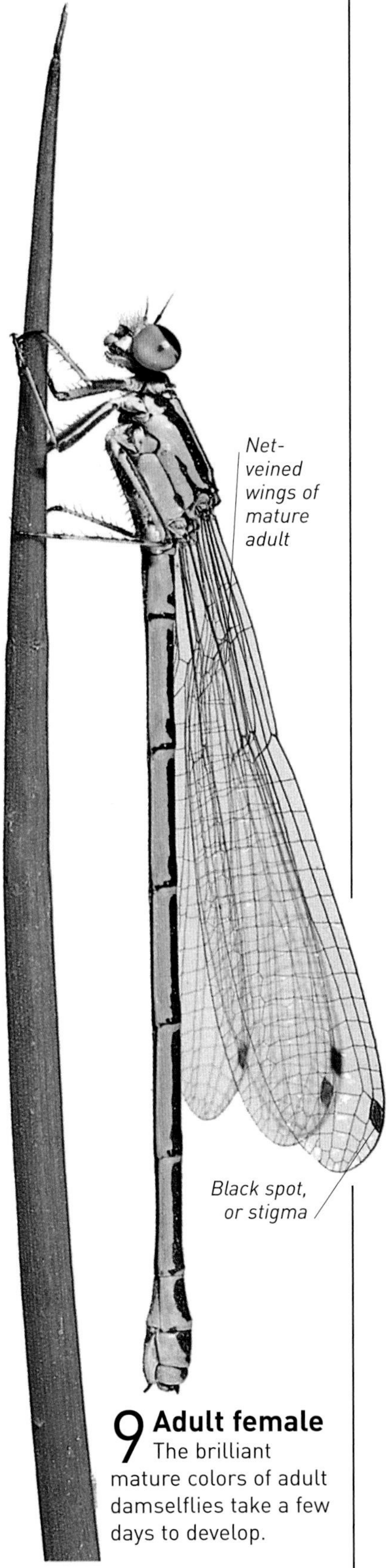

Net-veined wings of mature adult

Black spot, or stigma

9 Adult female

The brilliant mature colors of adult damselflies take a few days to develop.

Beetles

There are at least 300,000 different kinds of beetles, living everywhere from snowy mountain tops to scorching deserts. All beetles undergo complete metamorphosis. Their eggs hatch into grubs, some of which feed and grow for several years before becoming adults. Adult beetles are the most heavily armored of all insects. They have tough front wings that meet in the middle to protect the more delicate hind wings, which they use for flying. Beetles come in all sizes—from tiny fungus beetles smaller than a pinhead, to the giant Goliath up to 6 in (15 cm) long.

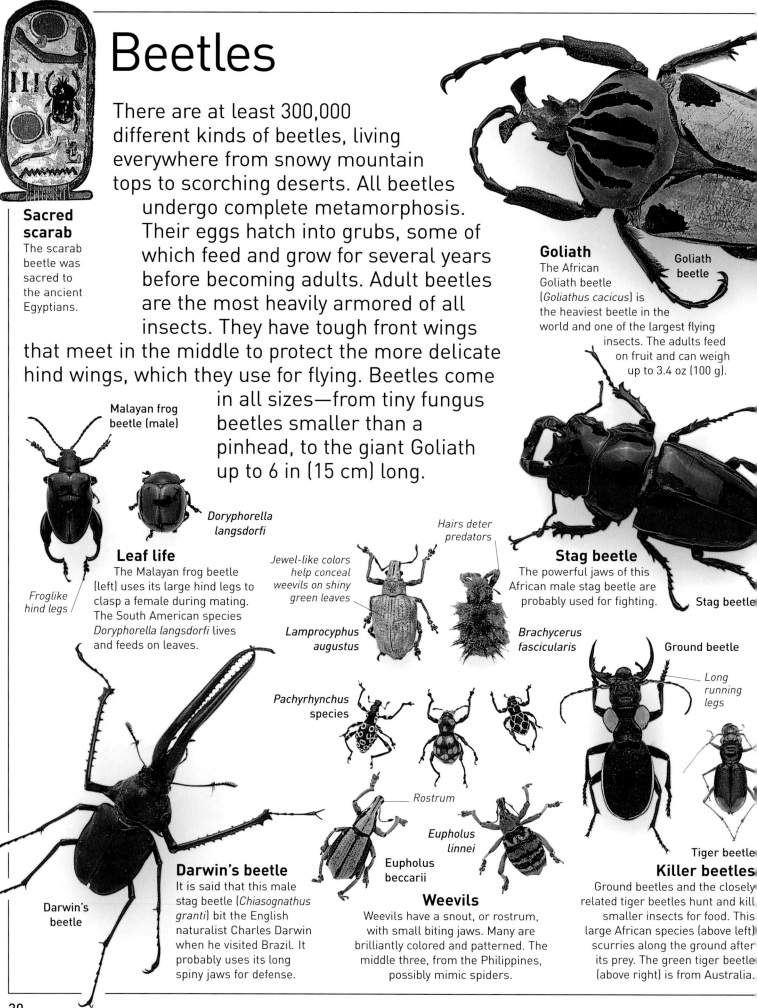

Sacred scarab
The scarab beetle was sacred to the ancient Egyptians.

Goliath
The African Goliath beetle (*Goliathus cacicus*) is the heaviest beetle in the world and one of the largest flying insects. The adults feed on fruit and can weigh up to 3.4 oz (100 g).

Goliath beetle

Malayan frog beetle (male)

Doryphorella langsdorfi

Leaf life
The Malayan frog beetle (left) uses its large hind legs to clasp a female during mating. The South American species *Doryphorella langsdorfi* lives and feeds on leaves.

Froglike hind legs

Jewel-like colors help conceal weevils on shiny green leaves

Hairs deter predators

Lamprocyphus augustus

Brachycerus fascicularis

Stag beetle
The powerful jaws of this African male stag beetle are probably used for fighting.

Stag beetle

Pachyrhynchus species

Ground beetle

Long running legs

Rostrum

Eupholus linnei

Eupholus beccarii

Darwin's beetle
It is said that this male stag beetle (*Chiasognathus granti*) bit the English naturalist Charles Darwin when he visited Brazil. It probably uses its long spiny jaws for defense.

Darwin's beetle

Weevils
Weevils have a snout, or rostrum, with small biting jaws. Many are brilliantly colored and patterned. The middle three, from the Philippines, possibly mimic spiders.

Tiger beetle

Killer beetles
Ground beetles and the closely related tiger beetles hunt and kill smaller insects for food. This large African species (above left) scurries along the ground after its prey. The green tiger beetle (above right) is from Australia.

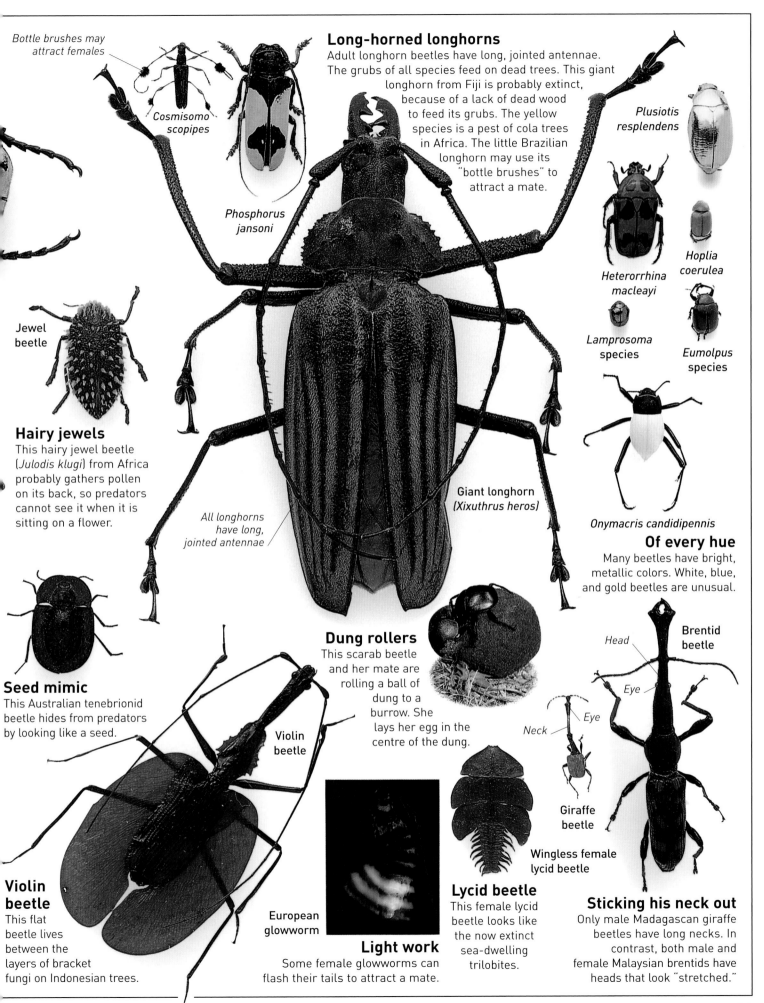

Bottle brushes may attract females

Cosmisomo scopipes

Phosphorus jansoni

Long-horned longhorns
Adult longhorn beetles have long, jointed antennae. The grubs of all species feed on dead trees. This giant longhorn from Fiji is probably extinct, because of a lack of dead wood to feed its grubs. The yellow species is a pest of cola trees in Africa. The little Brazilian longhorn may use its "bottle brushes" to attract a mate.

Plusiotis resplendens

Heterorrhina macleayi

Hoplia coerulea

Lamprosoma species

Eumolpus species

Jewel beetle

Hairy jewels
This hairy jewel beetle (*Julodis klugi*) from Africa probably gathers pollen on its back, so predators cannot see it when it is sitting on a flower.

All longhorns have long, jointed antennae

Giant longhorn (*Xixuthrus heros*)

Onymacris candidipennis

Of every hue
Many beetles have bright, metallic colors. White, blue, and gold beetles are unusual.

Seed mimic
This Australian tenebrionid beetle hides from predators by looking like a seed.

Violin beetle

Dung rollers
This scarab beetle and her mate are rolling a ball of dung to a burrow. She lays her egg in the centre of the dung.

Brentid beetle

Head

Eye

Eye

Neck

Giraffe beetle

Wingless female lycid beetle

Violin beetle
This flat beetle lives between the layers of bracket fungi on Indonesian trees.

European glowworm

Light work
Some female glowworms can flash their tails to attract a mate.

Lycid beetle
This female lycid beetle looks like the now extinct sea-dwelling trilobites.

Sticking his neck out
Only male Madagascan giraffe beetles have long necks. In contrast, both male and female Malaysian brentids have heads that look "stretched."

Flies

A fly is an insect with two wings. Instead of hind wings, flies have a pair of small structures called halteres, which help them balance in flight. Flies have large compound eyes, and claws and pads on their feet so they can walk on any surface. Some kinds of flies help humans by pollinating crops, but many, like mosquitoes, are pests that spread diseases, such as malaria, and carry germs. All flies undergo complete metamorphosis. The grubs, or maggots, live mainly in water or in moist, rotting plant and animal tissue.

No flies on me!
This unlucky character in the film *Return of the Fly* is gradually turning into a fly.

Wingless
This tiny bat fly (*Penicillidia fulvida*, above right) has no wings. It lives in the fur of bats and feeds on blood. The female gives birth to a fully grown grub.

European crane fly

Halteres used for balancing

The world's biggest crane fly

An eye for an eye
The stalked eyes of this male fly (*Achias rothschildi*, left) from New Guinea are used to threaten other males with shorter eye stalks.

Eye

Stalk-eyed fly

Beetle mimic
This small fly (*Celyphus hyacinthus*, left) from Malaysia looks remarkably like a beetle.

Soldierfly

Celyphus hyacinthus

Green skin
The green color of this South American soldierfly (*Hedriodiscus pulcher*, above) is caused by an unusual green pigment in the cuticle.

Long-legged crane flies
There are around 10,000 known species of crane fly, and the *Holorusia* species (right), from China, is one of the largest. The smaller species (*Ctenophora ornata*, above right) is from Europe. Crane fly maggots have such a tough covering that they are often called "leather-jackets."

A fasting fly
The grubs of this South American fly (*Pantophthalmus bellardii*, below) bore into living wood. Little is known about the large adults, and it may be that they do not even feed.

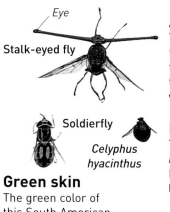

No eye stalks
This African fly (*Clitodoca fenestralis*, above) is related to the stalk-eyed fly from New Guinea. The patterned wings and red head may be important in courtship.

Dung fly

Housefly

Dung feeders
Dung flies are commonly seen on wet cow dung. Houseflies also breed on animal dung, as well as on decaying food. They are responsible for spreading many diseases.

Flesh eaters
When a mosquito carrying the eggs of a human warblefly feeds on a human, the eggs hatch and the larvae bore under the human's skin. Bluebottles are also common pests, breeding in rotting meat and dead bodies and spreading disease.

Human warblefly

Bluebottle

Drone flies

According to the Old Testament, Samson saw a swarm of bees in the dead body of a lion. The insects were almost certainly not bees, but yellow and black drone flies. These flies look like bees, but their larvae live and pupate in stagnant water.

African bee fly

The maggots of this African bee fly feed on developing grubs in wasps' nests.

Long tongue for feeding on nectar

Spider eater

The maggots of the *Lasia corvina* fly (above) feed on tarantulas.

A varied diet

This horsefly (above right) from Nepal feeds on blood, and has a long tongue to sip nectar.

A slim profile

Like true bees, this bee fly from Java sips nectar. Its larvae feed on live moth caterpillars.

Flat flower-feeder

This Argentinian fly (*Trichophthalma philippii*, below) feeds on nectar.

Short biting mouthparts

Long beelike tongue for sipping nectar

Bee-eating bee fly

This European bee fly (above) looks like a bumblebee. Its maggots eat grubs in the nests of solitary bees.

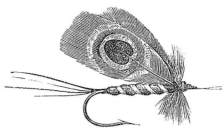

Fly fishing

Fishermen disguise their hooks with mock "flies" like this one (above), made from feathers and twine.

Tachinid flies

The maggots of tachinid flies feed on other insects while they are still alive. The yellowish species (*Paradejeeria rutiloides*, above left) from America attacks moth caterpillars. The green species (*Formosia moneta*, above right) from New Guinea feeds on scarab beetle larvae.

Syrphus torvus

Volucella zonaria

Hover flies

Hover flies have an amazing ability to hang in the air almost motionless, then suddenly dart away at speed. Many species have yellow and black stripes and look like wasps or bees. The maggots of the *Syrphus torvus* species feed on greenfly. *Volucella zonaria* maggots scavenge for food beneath wasps' nests.

This robber fly is feeding on an ichneumon fly

Mallophora atra

Pagidolaphria flammipennis

Blepharotes splendissimus

Pegesimallus teratodes

Plumed legs may help this fly attract his mate

Wing

Leg

Robber flies

These flies get their name from their habit of perching on suitable look-out points and attacking other insects flying past. They can be pests around bee hives, killing bees as they fly home. The large black species (*Mallophora atra*) from South America probably mimics carpenter bees. The male with plumed legs (*Pegesimallus teratodes*) is from Africa. He possibly waves his legs to try to attract a mate.

Largest fly

This South American mydid fly (*Mydas heros*, above) is probably the largest in the world. The maggots live in ants' nests, feeding on beetles—which are themselves scavenging on the rubbish left by the ants.

Butterflies and moths

Butterflies and moths form a single group of around 200,000 species. Generally, butterflies are brightly colored and fly during the day, whereas the more subtly colored moths are usually night-fliers. Most butterflies have clubbed antennae, while those of moths are usually straight or feathery. Adult butterflies and moths feed on liquids, which they suck up through a long, coiled tube called a "proboscis."

Jemadia hewitsonii

Hooked antenna

Amenis baroni

Butterfly or moth?
Skippers are halfway between butterflies and moths. Their antenna are thickened and hooked rather than clubbed like those of true butterflies

Nymphalid
The deep blue of this nymphalid butterfly is caused by the way the light strikes the tiny scales on its wings.

Geometrids
Many night-flying geometrid moths such as *Boarmia roboraria* (right) are pale colored. The bright colors of the *Milionia welskei* species (above) from Southeast Asia suggest that it flies during the day.

Feathery antenna

Don't eat me!
Red, yellow, and black colors often indicate that an insect is poisonous. This zygaenid moth (*Campylotes desgodinsi*, above) is probably avoided by birds.

Special legs
Some butterflies use their legs for cleaning their eyes.

Old lady moth
This old lady moth (*Mormo maura*) flies at night. During the day, its drab colors help to camouflage it.

Sunset moth

Uraniid moths
The uraniid moths live in the tropics. Many, like the Madagascan sunset moth (*Chrysiridia ripheus*, above) are day-flying and migrate long distances. Their brilliant colors are produced by scales on the wings that catch the light. The blue and white *Alcides aurora* species (right) is from New Guinea.

Alcides aurora

Hind wings look like fans

Featherlike moth antenna

Eyespot

End of a tail
The eyespots on the wings of this African moon moth (*Argema mimosae*, above) probably divert predators away from its delicate body. Similarly, the long tails will break off when attacked.

Long tails will break off if caught

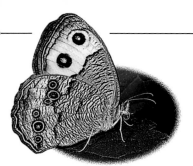

Butterflies rest with their wings folded together above their back

Underside

Upper side

Come in number 89!

These two photographs show both sides of the South American 89 butterfly (*Diaethria marchalii*). The blue wing spots disappear when the butterfly folds its wings.

Scent scales

Perfume for the lady

The male *Agrias claudina sardanapalus* butterfly (above) has yellow scent scales on its hind wings to attract females.

Transparent wings with very few scales

A see-through character

Cithaerias esmeralda (above) has see-through wings, making it a difficult target for predators.

Pupae

When a caterpillar has eaten enough, it turns into a pupa. As soon as this splits open, the adult emerges.

Under threat

The destruction of forests in Indonesia means this glass swallowtail species may soon die out.

Caterpillars

The eggs of butterflies and moths hatch into caterpillars.

Male birdwing butterfly

Abdomen

Tail deflects predators' attention from head

Swallowtail butterflies

The swallowtails get their name from their peculiarly extended hind wings that often look like the forked tail of a swallow. Because of its unusually clubbed hind wings, this common clubtail butterfly (*Pachliopta coon coon,* above) flies rather haphazardly and is often difficult to catch.

Metallic fleck

Metalmarks

Helicopis cupido has metallic flecks on its wings. Its 12 tails help to confuse predators.

Better red than dead

The underside of this red glider butterfly (*Cymothoe coccinata*) is brown, like a dead leaf.

Birdwing butterflies

The female of the species *Ornithoptera croesus* (right), is one of the largest butterflies in the world and spends most of her life high in the trees. The male is bright gold in color.

Female birdwing butterfly

Bugs

The word "bug" is often used to describe any crawling insect. But bugs are a special group of insects with a long, jointed feeding tube, specially adapted to piercing and sucking. The front wings of many bugs are hard and horny at the base, with thin, overlapping tips that protect the delicate hind wings. All bugs undergo incomplete metamorphosis, and young bugs look very similar to their parents, only without wings.

Curved rostrum (feeding tube)

Hissing assassin
Assassin bugs, like this species (*Rhinocoris alluaudi*), can produce hissing sounds by rasping their curved feeding tube against a structure under their body.

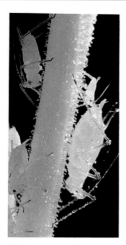

Who needs men!
Many aphids bear live young and can reproduce without the males.

Locris adult

Cuckoo-spit
"Cuckoo-spit" is froth produced by young froghoppers to protect them from drying out, and possibly from being eaten.

Frothy rain
This tree-living African froghopper (*Locris* species) produces so much froth that it falls to the ground like rain.

Leafhoppers
This *Graphocephala fennahi* leafhopper feeds on rhododendron leaves. Other species cause damage to a wide range of plants.

Bedbugs (enlarged)

Eye

Strong grasping front legs seize small water creatures

Bedbug (natural size)

Nighttime pests
The bedbug (*Cimex lectularius*) belongs to a small family of bloodsucking bugs, most of which live in the roosts and nests of bats and birds. They can live for several months without food.

Ceratocoris horni

Ground pearls
Many bugs are wingless and scarcely look like insects. These "ground pearls" are the skins of a group of plant-feeding bugs.

Ground pearls (*Margarodes formicarum*)

Spiny legs may be used for fighting

Spines may deter birds

Hemikyptha marginata

Scale insects (*Coccus hesperidum*)

Thasus acutangulus

Unusual plant feeders
Some plant-feeding bugs have unusual legs, like the spiny-legged bug (*Thasus acutangulus*). Others have horns, such as *Ceratocoris horni*, or strange shapes, such as *Hemikyptha marginata*.

Sap suckers
Wingless female mealybugs, scale insects, and ground pearls all feed on plant sap.

Mealybugs (*Planococcus citri*)

Serenading cicadas
Cicadas, like this Indian species (*Angamiana aetherea*, above), are known for the songs the males use to attract females. The nymphs live underground, sucking sap from plant roots.

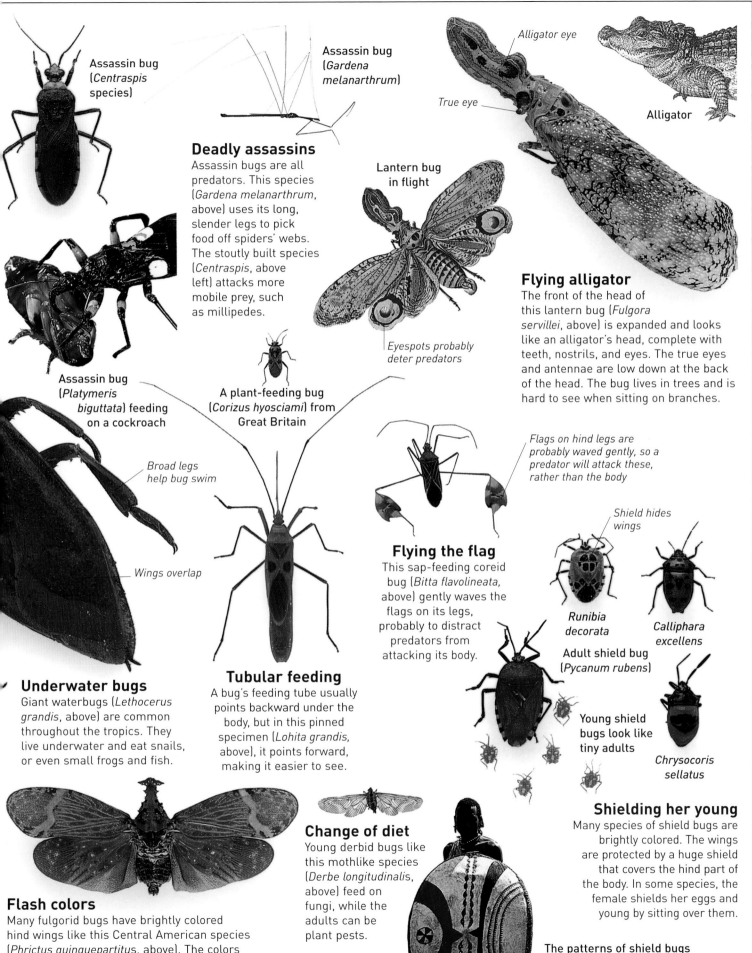

Assassin bug (*Centraspis* species)

Assassin bug (*Gardena melanarthrum*)

Alligator eye

True eye

Alligator

Deadly assassins
Assassin bugs are all predators. This species (*Gardena melanarthrum*, above) uses its long, slender legs to pick food off spiders' webs. The stoutly built species (*Centraspis*, above left) attacks more mobile prey, such as millipedes.

Lantern bug in flight

Eyespots probably deter predators

Flying alligator
The front of the head of this lantern bug (*Fulgora servillei*, above) is expanded and looks like an alligator's head, complete with teeth, nostrils, and eyes. The true eyes and antennae are low down at the back of the head. The bug lives in trees and is hard to see when sitting on branches.

Assassin bug (*Platymeris biguttata*) feeding on a cockroach

A plant-feeding bug (*Corizus hyosciami*) from Great Britain

Broad legs help bug swim

Wings overlap

Flags on hind legs are probably waved gently, so a predator will attack these, rather than the body

Shield hides wings

Runibia decorata

Calliphara excellens

Adult shield bug (*Pycanum rubens*)

Flying the flag
This sap-feeding coreid bug (*Bitta flavolineata*, above) gently waves the flags on its legs, probably to distract predators from attacking its body.

Young shield bugs look like tiny adults

Chrysocoris sellatus

Underwater bugs
Giant waterbugs (*Lethocerus grandis*, above) are common throughout the tropics. They live underwater and eat snails, or even small frogs and fish.

Tubular feeding
A bug's feeding tube usually points backward under the body, but in this pinned specimen (*Lohita grandis*, above), it points forward, making it easier to see.

Shielding her young
Many species of shield bugs are brightly colored. The wings are protected by a huge shield that covers the hind part of the body. In some species, the female shields her eggs and young by sitting over them.

Change of diet
Young derbid bugs like this mothlike species (*Derbe longitudinalis*, above) feed on fungi, while the adults can be plant pests.

Flash colors
Many fulgorid bugs have brightly colored hind wings like this Central American species (*Phrictus quinquepartitus*, above). The colors are probably flashed to startle predators.

The patterns of shield bugs resemble tribal shields

Wasps, bees, and ants

Wasps, bees, ants, and their relatives make up one of the largest groups of insects. Apart from sawflies, all wasps, bees, and ants can be recognized by their narrow "waist." At the end of the abdomen of many female wasps and bees, the egg-laying apparatus (ovipositor) is modified as a painful sting. Several species of wasps, bees, and ants are "social" insects that live together in a nest they build themselves. Since early times, humans have kept bees for honey. Many species of wasps are useful to farmers as they kill the grubs and caterpillars that destroy crops. Together with bees, they are important pollinators, ensuring that our fruit and vegetable crops flourish.

Male

Tree wasps
In summer, tree wasp workers kill caterpillars to feed their grubs. In fall, when there are no grubs to feed, they become household pests, seeking sugary foods.

Queen

Worker

Wasp waist
In the late 19th century, tiny "wasp waists" were the height of female fashion.

Sting injects poison, causing a painful wound

Sting
This is a magnified photograph of a sting—a modification of the ovipositor of many bees and wasps.

Hornet

Hornets
The hornet (*Vespa crabro*, left) is the largest wasp in Europe. The queen begins her nest in spring. Her first eggs hatch into female workers that provide food for the grubs and for the queen herself. Males are produced later.

Tarantula hawk

Spider killers
The tarantula hawk is the world's largest wasp. The female wasp paralyzes the spider with her sting, then lays an egg on its body. When the egg hatches, the grub has a ready supply of fresh spider meat.

Parasitic bee

Parasitic bee
This large blue species (*Aglae caerulea*, left) lays its eggs in the nests made by orchid bees (below). The developing grub then eats the orchid bee grub as well as its food store.

Perfume makers
Male orchid bees collect a substance from orchid flowers, which they convert into a scent to attract females.

Orchid bees

Euglossa assarophora

Euglossa intersecta

Biggest bee
This Asian carpenter bee is the world's largest bee. It makes nests in tunnels in rotting wood.

Bumblebees
Like honeybees, bumblebees are social insects and live in groups. This mountain bumblebee (*Bombus monticola*, above) nests in a burrow in the ground, often close to bilberry bushes.

Boring into trees

Female ichneumon wasps are parasitic—they lay their eggs on other insects, which the developing larvae consume. This female European rhyssine wasp (*Rhyssa persuasoria*, left) uses her long ovipositor to drill through wood to reach a live woodboring sawfly grub, on which she lays her egg.

Long ovipositor

Female has long abdomen for laying eggs

Male

Pelecinus polyturator wasps

Long abdomen

This female wasp (far left) has a long abdomen to allow her to reach into rotting wood and lay her eggs on beetle grubs.

Amblyteles wasp   Chrysalis

Cocoons of *Apanteles* wasp

Parasitic wasps

The *Apanteles gratiosus* wasp lays its eggs on hairy caterpillars. After the grubs have eaten the inside of the caterpillar, they form cocoons on the surface.

Fussy feeders

This European ichneumon wasp (*Amblyteles armatorius*, above) will only develop inside the chrysalis of one particular species of moth.

Eaten from within

A new generation of wasps will emerge from the cocoons on this hawk moth caterpillar.

Chalinus imperialis larvae feed on beetle grubs in wood

This giant wood wasp from Scandinavia is a pest of pine trees

Sawflies

Unlike other wasps, sawflies do not have a typical "waist." They owe their name to the sawlike blades of the egg-laying apparatus, or ovipositor, which the females use to insert eggs into plant tissues. The grubs, which often look like moth caterpillars, feed on plants. Sawflies are much less common in the tropics than in temperate parts of the world.

The *Cimbex femoratus* grub feeds on birch leaves

Butterfly hunter

The *Editha magnifica* wasp (above) from South America attacks butterflies as they sit in groups on the ground. The wasp stings the butterflies one at a time, bites off their wings, and stores the bodies in a burrow in which it lays its eggs. The developing grubs feed on the butterflies' bodies until they are large enough to pupate.

Ants

Ants live in colonies of up to 100,000 individuals. Their remarkably strong jaws can give a painful nip. When some species bite, they squirt formic acid from their abdomen into the wound—making it doubly painful.

Driver ant winged male, or "sausage fly"

Sausage fly

Male driver ants are often called "sausage flies," because of their long, fat bodies.

Chlorion lobatum

Dinoponera grandis

Driver ant workers

Driver ant queen

Driver ant

African driver ants form large colonies, but they have no permanent nests. They set up temporary camps while the queen lays eggs, and then they move on, taking the developing grubs with them.

Hunting wasps

Chlorion lobatum wasps sting crickets and then lay an egg on them. When the wasp egg hatches, the grub feeds on the cricket's body.

Largest ant

Dinoponera ants have the largest known workers. They live in small colonies, but are solitary hunters.

Ants communicate by touch and smell

Other insects

There are five main groups of insects: beetles, bugs, flies, wasps (including ants and bees), and butterflies and moths. However, there are another 25 similar, but smaller groups, such as the cockroaches, earwigs, ant lions, mantids, dragonflies, grasshoppers, and stick insects. There are also several groups of much smaller species, including various types of lice.

Jiminy Cricket
Curiously, Walt Disney's Jiminy Cricket has only two legs.

Stephens Island weta
These large crickets (below) are now almost extinct.

Stephens Island weta
(*Deinacrida rugosa*)

Eurycantha calcarata from Papua New Guinea

Antenna

Slender, jointed leg

Grasping front legs sometimes make the insect look as though it is praying

Strong hind legs enable fleas to jump great distances

Mating fleas

Living sticks
Stick insects usually have long, slender legs and antennae. During the day, they avoid predators by hanging almost motionless in shrubs and trees, looking just like another twig. At night, they move around to feed on leaves.

Praying mantid (*Sibylla pretiosa*) from Africa

Praying for food
Praying mantids feed on other insects, which they grasp in their specially adapted front legs.

Fleas
Adult fleas are all bloodsuckers. Each kind of flea prefers the blood of one kind of bird or animal. An animal flea will only attack a human if it is very hungry. The tiny, white flea larvae do not feed on blood, but on decaying material in nests and carpets.

Colors help conceal cricket on lichen-covered branches

Wing

Anchiale maculata from New Guinea

Spines protect against attack

Singing
Male grasshoppers, like the African *Physemacris variolosa* (right), produce sounds to attract females by rubbing their hind legs against their front wings. In contrast, crickets, such as the Malaysian species *Trachyzulpha fruhstorferi* (far right), "sing" by rubbing the two front wings together.

Grasshopper's abdomen expands to act as a drum

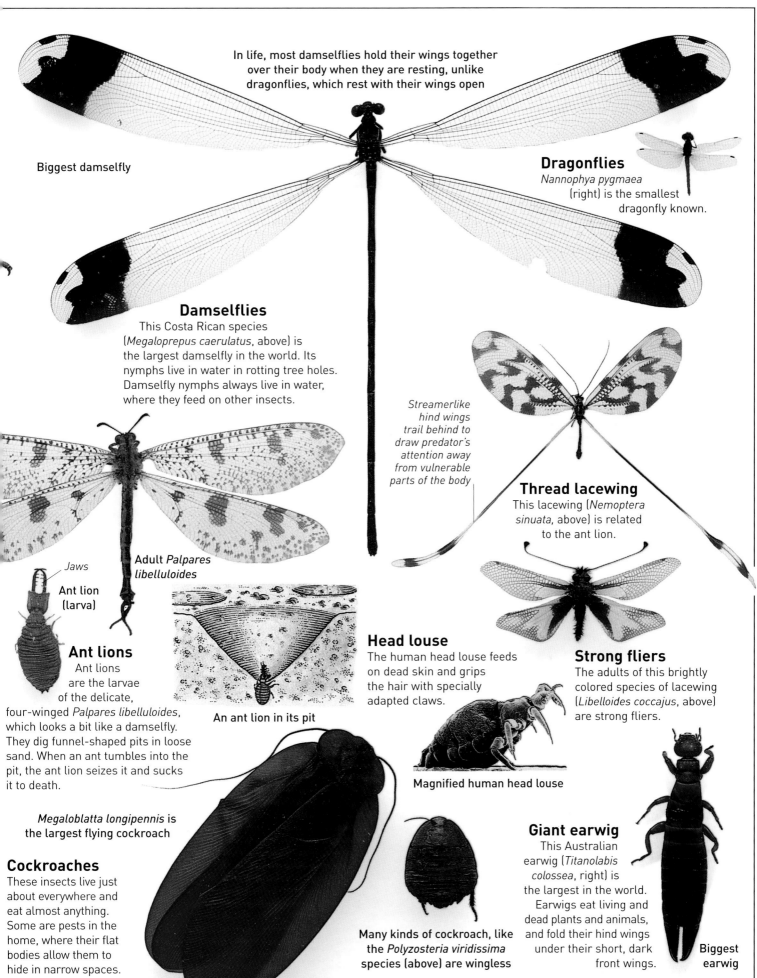

In life, most damselflies hold their wings together over their body when they are resting, unlike dragonflies, which rest with their wings open

Biggest damselfly

Dragonflies
Nannophya pygmaea (right) is the smallest dragonfly known.

Damselflies
This Costa Rican species (*Megaloprepus caerulatus*, above) is the largest damselfly in the world. Its nymphs live in water in rotting tree holes. Damselfly nymphs always live in water, where they feed on other insects.

Streamerlike hind wings trail behind to draw predator's attention away from vulnerable parts of the body

Thread lacewing
This lacewing (*Nemoptera sinuata*, above) is related to the ant lion.

Jaws

Ant lion (larva)

Adult *Palpares libelluloides*

Ant lions
Ant lions are the larvae of the delicate, four-winged *Palpares libelluloides*, which looks a bit like a damselfly. They dig funnel-shaped pits in loose sand. When an ant tumbles into the pit, the ant lion seizes it and sucks it to death.

An ant lion in its pit

Head louse
The human head louse feeds on dead skin and grips the hair with specially adapted claws.

Strong fliers
The adults of this brightly colored species of lacewing (*Libelloides coccajus*, above) are strong fliers.

Magnified human head louse

Megaloblatta longipennis is the largest flying cockroach

Cockroaches
These insects live just about everywhere and eat almost anything. Some are pests in the home, where their flat bodies allow them to hide in narrow spaces.

Many kinds of cockroach, like the *Polyzosteria viridissima* species (above) are wingless

Giant earwig
This Australian earwig (*Titanolabis colossea*, right) is the largest in the world. Earwigs eat living and dead plants and animals, and fold their hind wings under their short, dark front wings.

Biggest earwig

Living with plants

In the coal forests that covered Earth more than 300 million years ago, there were few kinds of insects. Dragonflies flew around the swampy areas, but butterflies, bugs, and beetles had not yet evolved. The evolution of flowers and other types of plants encouraged the evolution of many new insect species. Some evolved as pollinators; others fed on buds and seeds or on the many different types of leaves and fruit that gradually became available. Equally important was the evolution of insects that live on dead plants and so restore nutrients to the soil.

Female gall

Male galls

Nail galls
Eucalyptus trees often produce growths called galls, in which mealybug grubs develop. When mature, the female inside the gall is fertilized by a male through a tiny hole. Males develop in nail-like galls that often grow on a female gall.

Beetle

Young adult beetle

Beetle gall cut open

Beetle gall
These *Sagra femorata* beetles developed inside the swollen stem of a climbing plant. The swelling started when the female beetle laid her eggs in the stem.

Flowers
Many flowers rely on insects for pollination.

Tunnel caused by fly grub

Black lines are the droppings produced by the grub as it eats its way along the leaf

Leaf miners
The twisting trails on this leaf are caused by the grubs of the *Phytomyza vitalbiae* fly. Each grub feeds on the tissue between the upper and lower surface of the leaf. As it eats, it tunnels out a shallow mine, leaving a trail of droppings behind. The grubs cause noticeable damage to green leaves and can eventually kill a healthy plant.

Healthy green leaf attacked by leaf miners

1 A clean bumblebee
Bees are essential to plants for carrying pollen from one flower to another, so ensuring that seeds are produced. This bumblebee, attracted by the sweet scent of the dog rose, lands to feed on pollen and sugary nectar.

2 Dusted with golden pollen
As the bee sucks the nectar using its long tongue, its hairy coat picks up grains of pollen from the stamens.

Pollen grains on stamens of flower

Yellow specks are pollen grains

Yew tree galls

When gall midges feed on yew trees, they cause the buds to stop growing and produce a ball of small leaves. Each gall contains a single gall midge grub (*Taxomyia taxi*).

Normal yew shoot

Yew gall *Yew gall*

Marbles on oak trees

Oak marble galls are common on oak trees in Europe. They are produced by the females of a small gall wasp (*Andricus kollari*).

Oak marble gall

Cherries on oak trees

When the gall wasp (*Cynips quercusfolii*) lays an egg in the vein of an oak leaf, a cherry gall grows to protect the developing grub.

Young gall is white

Rose galls

Rose galls are produced when a tiny gall wasp (*Diplolepis rosae*, above) lays her eggs on rosebuds in spring.

Pistachio galls

These tubular galls are produced by pistachio trees around colonies of a particular aphid (*Baizongia pistaciae*) in the Mediterranean region.

Pistachio gall

Leaf

Wind roses

Centuries ago in Persia, people believed that these pinkish galls came on the wind and called them "wind roses."

Currant gall cut in half

Gall

Grub inside gall

Cherry galls on oak leaf

Young grub

Mature grub

Cherry gall cycle

In winter, female gall wasps lay eggs on oak tree buds and galls develop. In late spring, grubs hatch and then they mate. The females lay eggs, and new cherry galls are produced.

3 Fill your baskets

As the bumblebee collects more and more pollen grains, it combs them from its body, packs them into the hairy pollen baskets on its hind legs, and then flies off to its nest.

Safe and sound

Some caterpillars roll up a leaf, fix it with silk, and then pupate safely hidden inside.

Silk strands

Oak currants

In spring, female gall wasps (*Neuroterus quercusbaccarum*) lay eggs on oak catkins, producing currant galls. The grubs hatch and, in summer, after mating, the females lay eggs on oak leaves. A flat, reddish cushion called a spangle gall forms around each egg. In spring, an all-female generation of wasps emerges and the cycle begins again.

Pollen packed into tiny baskets on hind legs

Oak apples

Oak apple galls form when a wingless female gall wasp (*Biorhiza pallida*) lays her eggs on an oak leaf bud. Winged males and females hatch from separate galls; these mate and the females lay eggs on the tree roots. The emerging females are wingless and have to climb up the oak trees to lay their eggs on the buds in order to produce next year's oak apples.

Oak apple

Hide and seek

Insects are eaten by many other animals, including birds, bats, frogs, lizards, and shrews. Many insects themselves hunt and kill other insects for food, and some insects are even eaten by people. With this range of predators, it is not surprising that many insects have developed unusual colors, patterns, and shapes to protect themselves. Some insects have mottled wings to match the color of tree bark. Leaf and stick insects are so well disguised as leaves and twigs that they are ignored by would-be predators.

Leaf me alone!
Some stick insects protect themselves by looking like leaves. They have leaflike wings and legs with flattened plates to break up their outline.

Flatid bug

Bark bugs
This Central American species of flatid bug (*Flatoides dealbatus*) sits on the bark of trees, where its light brown coloring makes it difficult to see. Some species are see-through, or translucent, while others have mottled brown and gray patches to blend in with lichen-covered trees.

Playing dead
This bush cricket (*Ommatoptera pictifolia*, below) from Brazil hides by standing quite still on a twig. Even the most bright-eyed predator would be fooled into thinking it was a dead leaf—it even seems to have leaf veins.

Antennae held flat against bark

Click beetle on bark
The whitish patches on the body of this click beetle help it blend in with the lichen on the bark of the tree.

Veins on wings look like veins on a leaf

Wings blend in with bark

Egg-laying apparatus (ovipositor)

Legs hold body in a leaflike position

Slightly tattered wings break insectlike outline, making it look like an old dead leaf

Bark mimic
When it sits pressed closely against a small branch, this grayish-brown bush cricket (*Sathrophyllia rugosa*, above) from India looks just like a piece of bark.

Break up the borders
An important role of camouflage is to disrupt the outline of a familiar object so that it is more difficult to see. Many insects, like this mantid (*Gongylus gongylodes*, above), have flattened plates on their body and legs that help to camouflage them.

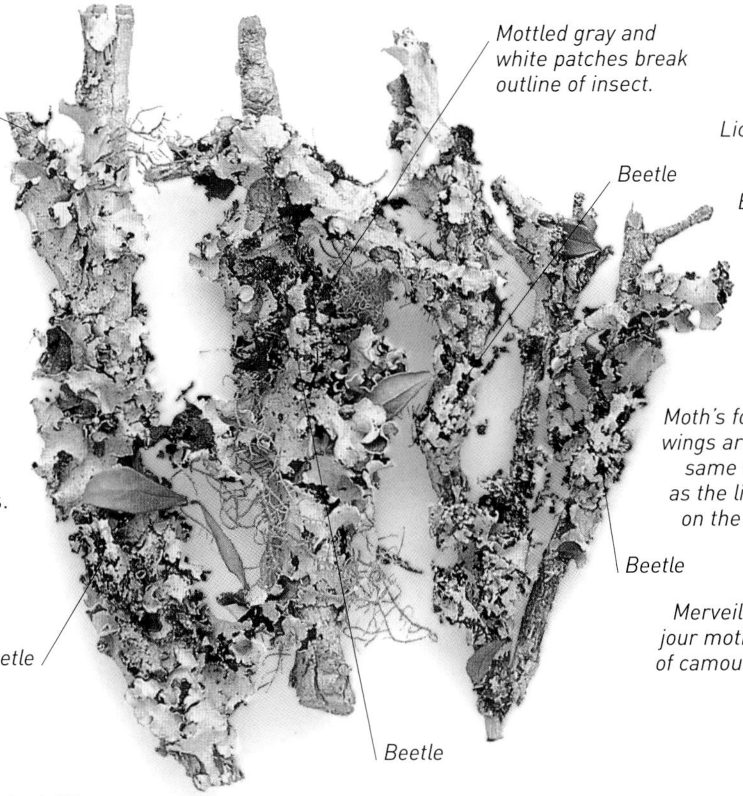

Lichen is a kind of plant that grows on tree trunks and on twigs.

Mottled gray and white patches break outline of insect.

Lichen

Beetle

Bark

Lichen longhorns

This Madagascan species of longhorn (*Lithinus nigrocristatus*, above) is remarkable for its ability to hide on lichen-covered twigs. It is almost impossible to see the four beetles hidden on the right.

Moth's folded wings are the same color as the lichen on the bark

Beetle

Merveille du jour moth out of camouflage

Beetle

Beetle

Merveille du jour moth

Many night-flying moths that spend their days resting on bark are well camouflaged against birds and lizards. Like the lichen longhorns, this merveille du jour moth (*Dichonia aprilina*, above) disappears from view in its natural habitat of lichen-covered trees. Out of camouflage, it is much easier to spot.

Camouflaged sticks

Live stick insects are almost invisible when sitting still on leaves and twigs. Occasionally, some stick and leaf insects will gently sway from side to side, so all a predator sees is just another leaf or twig caught by the breeze.

Winged male of Macleay's spectre (Extatosoma tiaratum) from Australia

Spiny green nymph (Eurycantha calcarata)

Short-winged female of Macleay's spectre (Extatosoma tiaratum)

Adult female green Indian stick insect (Carausius morosus)

Sticklike, green legs

Adult female pink-winged stick insect (Sipyloidea sipylus)

Avoiding predators

Hiding from predators is the key to survival for many insect species. Some insects use camouflage to blend in with their surroundings; others protect themselves with clearly visible spines, bright, flashing colors, strong, biting jaws, or powerful, kicking legs. Some quite harmless insects look and behave like poisonous or stinging creatures, so predators will mistake them for the real thing. After a nasty experience, hungry predators soon learn to leave unpleasant-tasting insects alone, and will avoid anything that could give them a painful bite or sting.

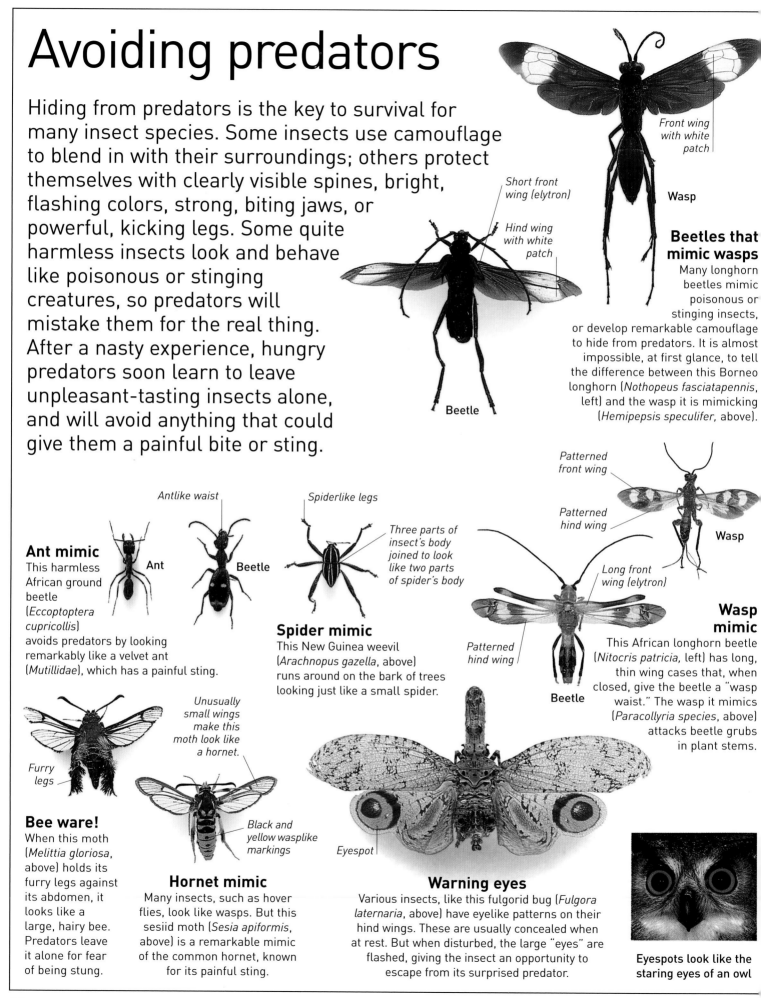

Front wing with white patch

Wasp

Short front wing (elytron)

Hind wing with white patch

Beetle

Beetles that mimic wasps

Many longhorn beetles mimic poisonous or stinging insects, or develop remarkable camouflage to hide from predators. It is almost impossible, at first glance, to tell the difference between this Borneo longhorn (*Nothopeus fasciatapennis*, left) and the wasp it is mimicking (*Hemipepsis speculifer*, above).

Antlike waist

Spiderlike legs

Three parts of insect's body joined to look like two parts of spider's body

Patterned front wing

Patterned hind wing

Wasp

Ant mimic
This harmless African ground beetle (*Eccoptoptera cupricollis*) avoids predators by looking remarkably like a velvet ant (*Mutillidae*), which has a painful sting.

Ant

Beetle

Spider mimic
This New Guinea weevil (*Arachnopus gazella*, above) runs around on the bark of trees looking just like a small spider.

Long front wing (elytron)

Patterned hind wing

Beetle

Wasp mimic
This African longhorn beetle (*Nitocris patricia*, left) has long, thin wing cases that, when closed, give the beetle a "wasp waist." The wasp it mimics (*Paracollyria* species, above) attacks beetle grubs in plant stems.

Furry legs

Unusually small wings make this moth look like a hornet.

Black and yellow wasplike markings

Eyespot

Bee ware!
When this moth (*Melittia gloriosa*, above) holds its furry legs against its abdomen, it looks like a large, hairy bee. Predators leave it alone for fear of being stung.

Hornet mimic
Many insects, such as hover flies, look like wasps. But this sesiid moth (*Sesia apiformis*, above) is a remarkable mimic of the common hornet, known for its painful sting.

Warning eyes
Various insects, like this fulgorid bug (*Fulgora laternaria*, above) have eyelike patterns on their hind wings. These are usually concealed when at rest. But when disturbed, the large "eyes" are flashed, giving the insect an opportunity to escape from its surprised predator.

Eyespots look like the staring eyes of an owl

Chemical gun

When a bombardier beetle is disturbed, it produces a sudden explosion of chemicals that frightens away predators.

Snake in the grass

Some caterpillars trick predators into thinking they are poisonous snakes. When alarmed, this hawkmoth caterpillar (*Leucorhampha ornatus*) rears its head and inflates its thorax to look like a snake's head.

Inflated thorax

False snake eye

Small postman butterfly (*Heliconius erato*) from southern Ecuador

Small postman butterfly (*Heliconius erato*) from western Brazil

Small postman butterfly (*Heliconius erato*) from southern Brazil

Rings of mimics

Some butterflies feed on rather poisonous plants. As a result, they taste unpleasant and are avoided by insect-eating birds. Different species may take advantage of this by mimicking each other's colors. These six butterflies represent two species from three different parts of South America.

Postman butterfly (*Heliconius melpomene*) from western Brazil

Postman butterfly (*Heliconius melpomene*) from southern Brazil

Postman butterfly (*Heliconius melpomene*) from southern Ecuador

Long, slender antenna

Egg-laying apparatus, or ovipositor

Spiny hind legs raised to frighten or injure predator

Feeding, not fighting

The spines and large jaws on this cricket (above) are used to hold and eat prey, but they will also deter predators.

Spiny hind legs

1 Warning weta

Because the wildlife in New Zealand developed without any mammals, a group of crickets called weta filled the role of the ground-living predators, eating a diet similar to that of shrews. These huge insects are now almost extinct.

2 Stick 'em up!

When disturbed, this species (*Hemideina thoracica*, above) raises its hind legs into a threatening posture. The spines on the legs can cause a nasty wound when the insect kicks.

A watery life

In order to breathe, water insects either swim to the surface for air, or extract air from the water, like fish. Some insects, such as dragonflies and many true flies, take advantage of the food supplies in water for their feeding and growing phase. As adults, they become winged and independent of water. Other insects have adapted to water and spend their entire life cycle there.

Mayfly adult

Skating
Pond skaters feed on drowning insects.

Prey is held in front four legs

Oarlike hind legs

Sucking mouthparts

Eye

Silvery film of air around body

Hairs help bug swim

Pincerlike legs

Surface hunters
Water boatmen (*Notonecta glauca*, above) are predatory bugs that swim upside-down just beneath the surface, attacking other insects that have fallen in. They come to the surface to breathe.

Saucer bugs
Saucer bugs (*Ilyocoris cimicoides*, left) have strong front legs for grasping their prey.

Air film
The silvery underside of a saucer bug (above) is caused by a film of air trapped beneath tiny hairs.

Strong, pincerlike front legs

Air is stored beneath the wings

Fringes on legs propel beetle through water

Giant water bug
This giant water bug (below), shown smaller than life-size, was drawn by Maria Merian in 1700.

Gills extract oxygen from water

Predatory damsel
Damselfly nymphs (left) breathe through external gills on the tip of the abdomen.

Diving beetles
Great diving beetles (*Dytiscus marginalis*, above) are fierce predators. Like water boatmen, they store air under their wings.

Segmented antenna

Strong, grasping front legs

Suckerlike pads used in mating

Caddis fly larva
Many caddis fly larvae spin a tube of silk, on to which they stick stones, sand, or bits of plant for camouflage.

Pieces of plant

Sticks and stones

Caddis fly larvae

Water beetle pupa
The larva of the great diving beetle (below right) crawls out of the pond and burrows into damp soil, where it pupates.

Adult dragonfly

With their bright colors flashing in the sun, dragonflies hover above the water, ready to dart after their insect prey.

Dragonflies emerging

When they are big enough, the wingless dragonfly nymphs crawl out of the water. They then emerge from their nymphal skin as winged adults.

Siphons take in air

A measured pace

The water measurer (*Hydrometra stagnorum*, below) walks on the water's surface, feeding on dead insects.

Water siphons

Mosquito larvae (*Culex* species, left) have no legs, but can swim by wriggling sharply. They come to the surface to breathe, drawing in air through a siphon at the tip of the abdomen.

Long antenna

Vibrating brushes waft food particles into the mouth

Water beetle larva

The great diving beetle larva pumps digestive juices into its prey through pointed jaws. It then sucks in the digested body contents.

Fringed, oarlike hind leg

Pointed, tubular jaws

Dragonfly eggs form sticky groups on plants for several days

Dragonfly nymphs have no external gills.

Egg surrounded by jelly

Lesser boatmen

Lesser water boatmen (above) are often found in polluted water, where they feed on decaying plants and animals.

Dragonfly nymphs may take two to three years to grow to adult size. They eat small fish and tadpoles.

Dragonfly nymph

Sharp hooks

Midges

Chironomids (non-biting midges) are tiny flies that fly in swarms near water. The larvae feed on bacteria and help to dispose of human waste in sewage plants.

Midge larva

Mask extended

Mask

The dragonfly nymph's lower lip is expanded into a hinged structure called a mask. This shoots out to grasp prey and draw it back to the jaws.

Mask

The Mayfly nymph breathes through feathery gills on its back.

Building a nest

The start
The common wasp queen starts a nest by building a short stalk with a cap, covering a comb of four or five cells. She lays one egg at the bottom of each cell.

The nests of the common wasp (*Vespula vulgaris*) are started by a single queen working on her own. She builds each nest from chewed-up wood fibers and lays her eggs inside. The emerging grubs become the first workers—they expand the nest and forage for food, so that the queen can stay in the nest to lay more eggs.

Stalk

New envelope is built down and around older envelopes

1 Insulating layers
The queen builds a series of envelopes around her small comb to insulate the larvae from cold winds. The nests of the common wasp are always built with the entrance at the bottom, unlike some tropical wasps' nests.

The queen lays one egg at the bottom of each paper cell.

Caring for the eggs
When the eggs hatch, the queen must collect food for her grubs as well as more material to extend the nest walls.

3 Keeping guard
The nest entrance is now just a small hole. This is easier to defend from other insects, including other queens who might try to take over the nest.

Developing grub in its own cell

2 The white house
This queen has found a source of nesting material that is almost white. She chews away some wood fibers to make the "paper" from which she builds the nest.

Paper cells made by queen

Larvae
On their rich diet of chewed insects and caterpillars, the grubs grow quickly. The time from egg to adult is usually about five weeks.

The queen uses her antennae to measure the envelopes and cells

White paper envelopes are made from fibers of wood, which the queen chews and mixes with saliva to make a sort of "paper."

Entrance to nest is small to protect the larvae inside, and to help control the temperature and humidity

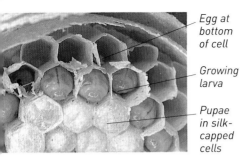

Egg at bottom of cell

Growing larva

Pupae in silk-capped cells

Grubs with caps on

Just before the larvae pupate, they spin their own silken cap to close their cell. A few days later, the first set of workers emerges.

4 Change of color

The first workers start to collect wood fibers from many different sources, and so the "paper" they make is often multicolored. Inside the nest, the old paper envelopes are chewed away to make room for larger combs of cells.

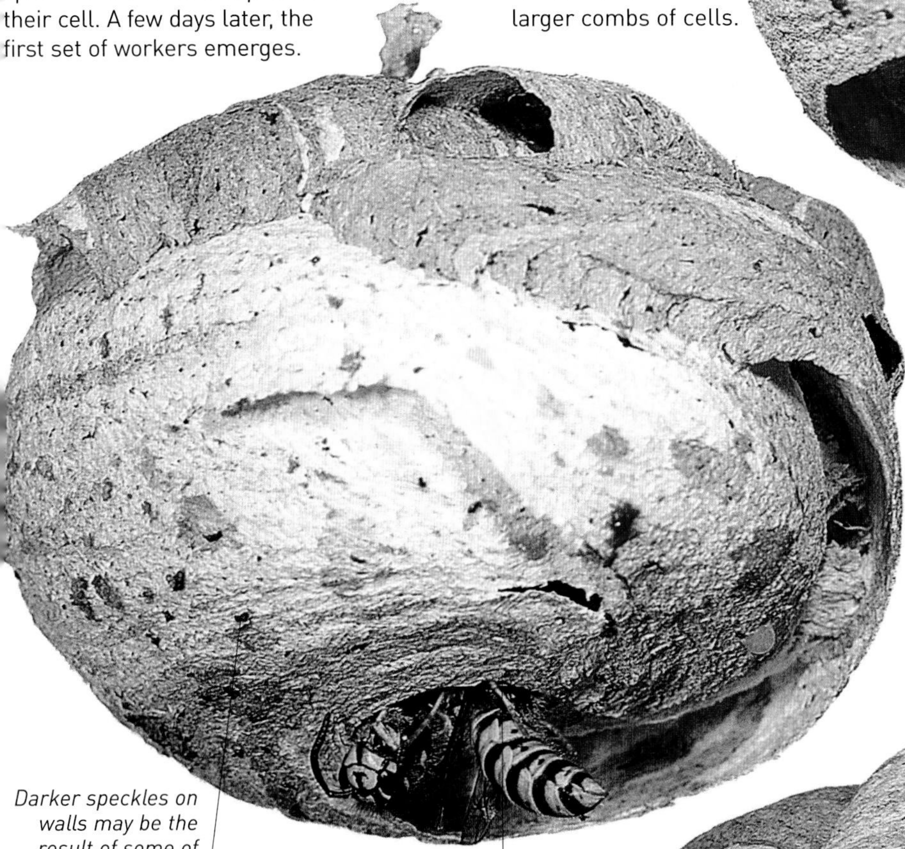

5 How many wasps?

A large nest may contain more than 500 adult wasps in summer. Between spring and fall, it will produce several thousand individuals, most of whom die from exhaustion.

Cross-section

This old engraving shows how the envelopes surround the comb of cells in a young nest. Older nests will have four or five horizontal combs.

Darker speckles on walls may be the result of some of the workers having fed on treated wood

Different types of wood, making the paper multicolored

Underground nests

The common wasp often builds nests underground. As the nest grows, the workers have to dig away soil and stones to provide more room.

6 The next generation

In summer, the wasps build several larger cells. The grubs in these cells are given extra food. These larger grubs develop into males and queens, which fly from the nest and mate.

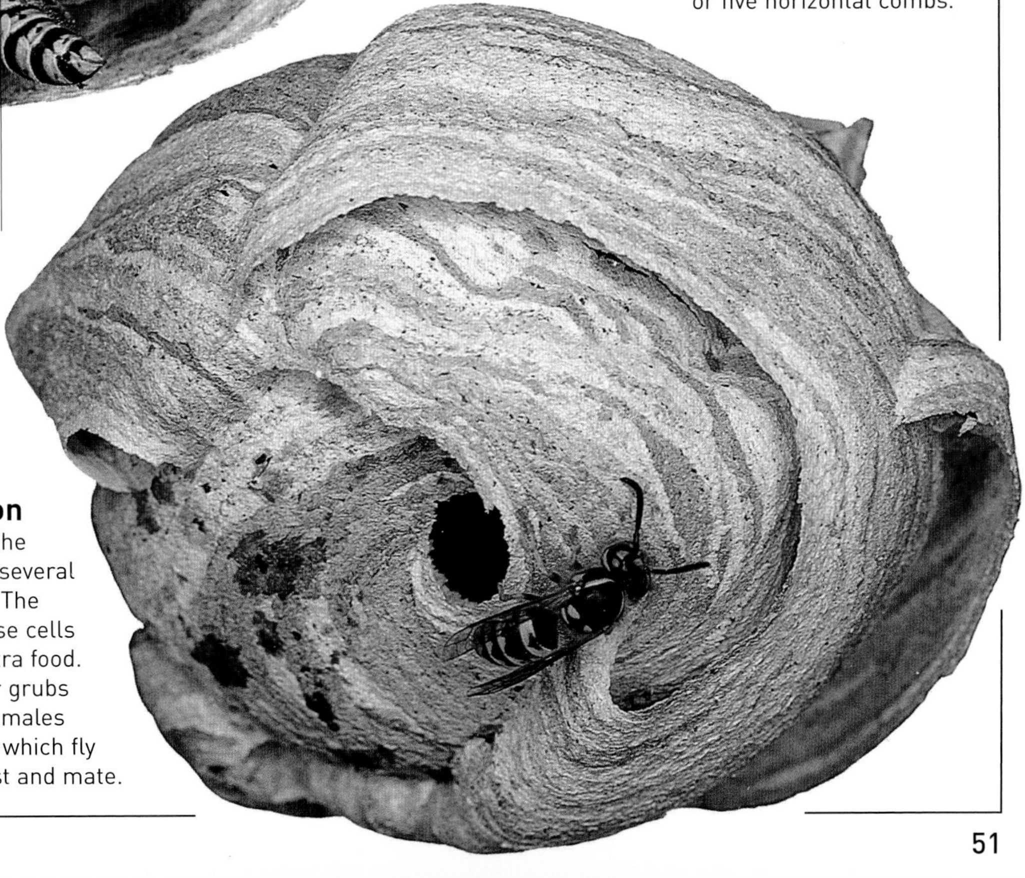

51

Insect architects

Wasps, bees, ants, and termites build a wide range of nests to protect their young. The simplest is a burrow in the soil made by a solitary wasp. The most complex is made by termites and contains millions of workers and a single queen. Some nests, like those built by common wasps and honeybees, are started by a single queen. Others are started by swarms of female wasps, sometimes with several queens.

Long and thin
Ropalidia wasps build simple, open nests. Each consists of only a few cells hanging from a central stalk. The female lays a single egg in each cell and feeds the grubs as they develop.

Open house
These open nests (above) are built in warm countries by *Polistes* wasps.

Hole where branch was

Leaf

Vertical combs

Job sharing
African *Belanogaster* wasps build exposed combs with long cells. Each nest is started by one female who is joined later by several others.

Leafy nest
Protopolybia sedula, a South American wasp species, builds a nest of up to 10 vertical combs between the leaves of a plant (above).

Walls are made largely of hardened mud, which the workers pick up wet from the sides of streams

Clay nest
The nest of *Polybia singularis* is built largely of mud. As each nest is so heavy, it must be hung from a stout branch.

Mud vase
Oriental *Stenogaster* wasps produce attractive vaselike nests made of mud and plant fibers (above). Each nest is built by a solitary female.

Vertical slitlike entry hole is unique to this species of wasp

Paper cones

The cylindrical nests of the South American *Chartergus globiventris* wasp have a small entry hole at the bottom. The nests vary in size from about 2 in (5 cm) long and 1.2 in (3 cm) wide to 3 ft (100 cm) long and 6 in (15 cm) wide. The largest nests contain many thousands of wasps with several egg-laying queens.

Entrance hole

Hole at the center of each level allows wasps to move from floor to floor

Entrance hole

Spiny nest

The *Polybia scutellaris* wasp from Argentina and southern Brazil makes its nest from chewed plant fibers. The outer envelope is covered with hard papery spines.

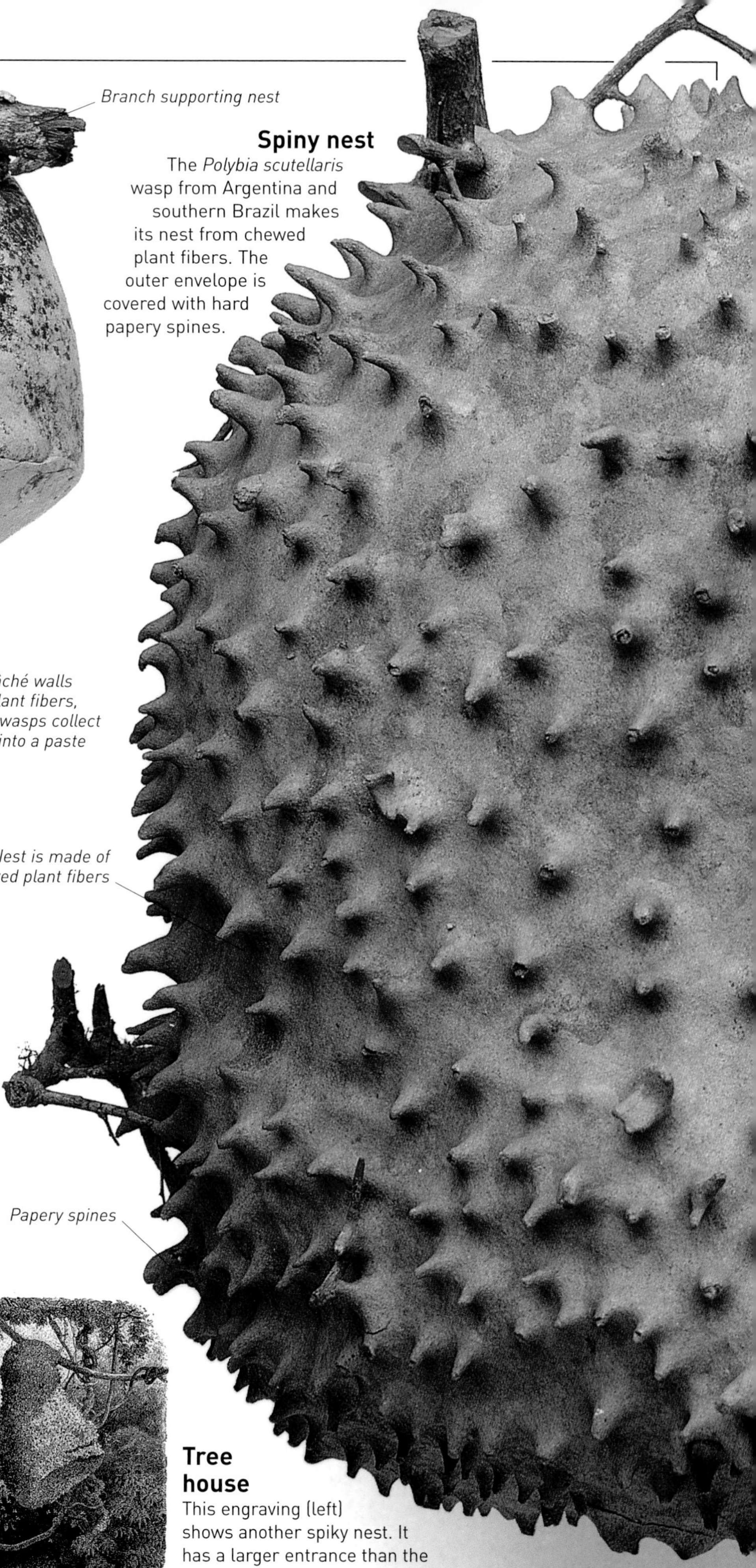

Branch supporting nest

Papier-mâché walls made of plant fibers, which the wasps collect and chew into a paste

Nest is made of chewed plant fibers

Papery spines

Carton nest

The nest above has been cut in half to show the inside. It is built from plant fibers, which the adult wasps collect and chew into a paste like papier mâché. They build several layers of combs to rear their young, with a hole at the center of each layer, so they can easily move from "floor" to "floor."

Tree house

This engraving (left) shows another spiky nest. It has a larger entrance than the *Polybia scutellaris* nest above.

Continued on next page   53

Continued from previous page

Nest of *Polybia scutellaris* from South America

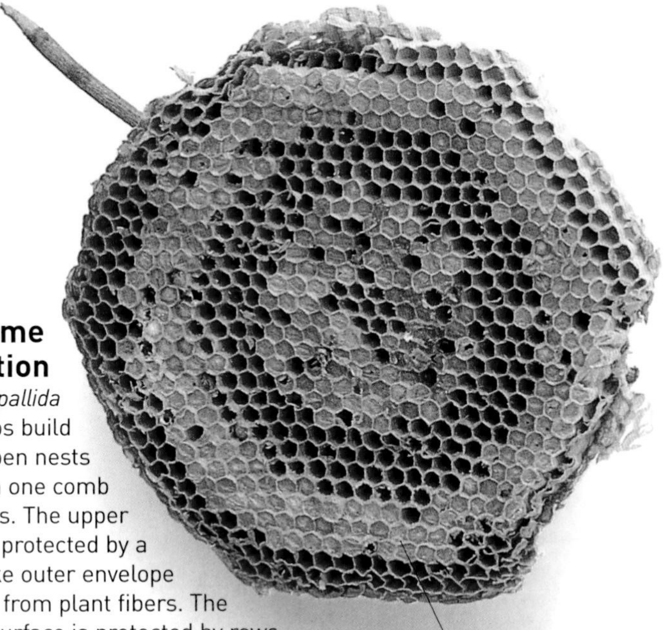

Home protection

Apoica pallida wasps build simple open nests (right) with one comb of cells. The upper surface is protected by a conelike outer envelope made from plant fibers. The lower surface is protected by rows of wasps, all facing outward to ward off predators.

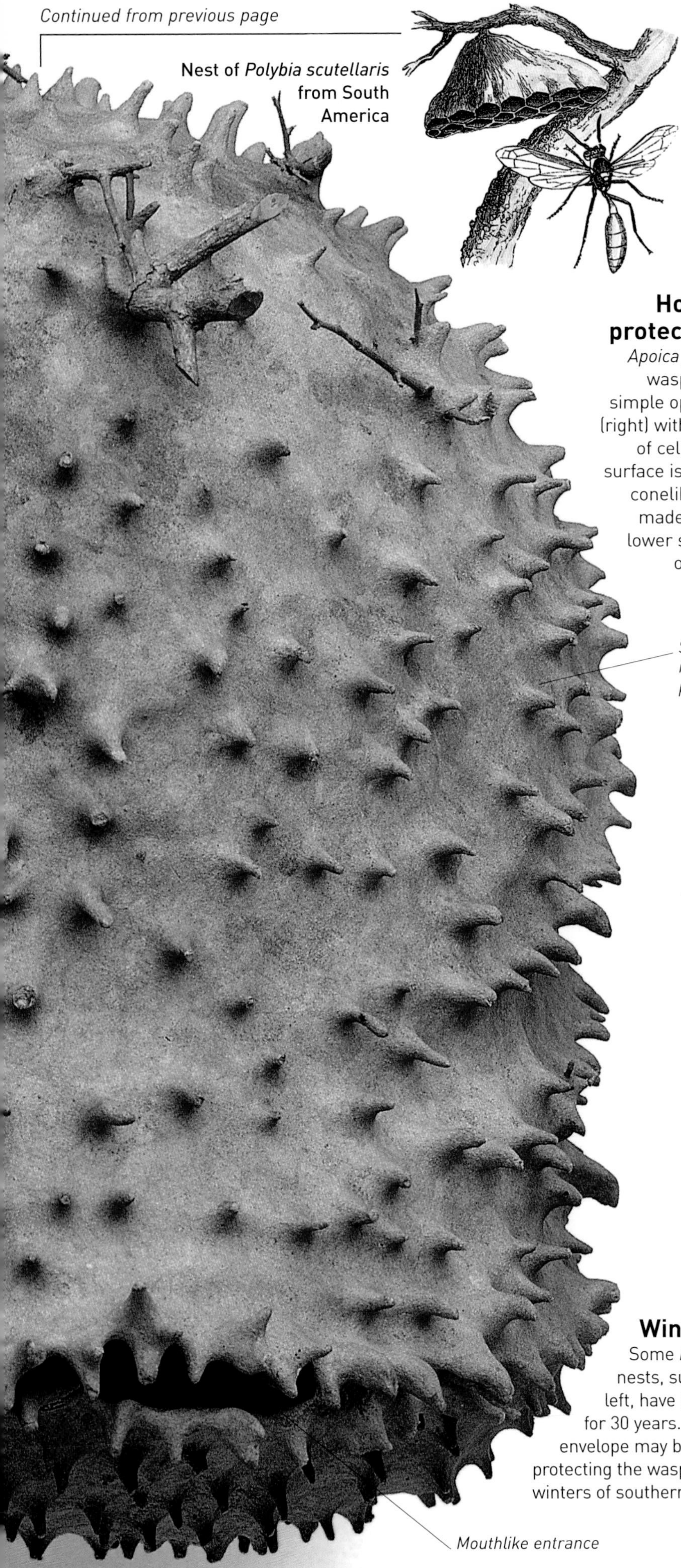

Brood cells containing developing grubs

Spiny outer casing is made of chewed plant fibers

Entrance to nest

Drummers' home

This simple nest with a single comb (right) is produced by a swarm of wasps that is thought to include several queens. These metallic blue wasps (*Synoeca surinama*) are among the largest social wasps in South America. They fly quietly, but when annoyed, they drum on the inside of their nest to produce a warning sound.

Winter protection

Some *Polybia scutellaris* nests, such as the one on the left, have been known to exist for 30 years. The thick, spiny envelope may be important in protecting the wasps through the cooler winters of southern South America.

Mouthlike entrance

Tree termites

Many termites build nests in trees, although these are usually connected to other parts of the same colony, either underground or in other trees. Termites make communicating galleries with roofs by sticking soil particles together, or they tunnel in wood or underground.

Termites

The biggest and most complex insect societies are built by termites. The nests of some species, like the west African *Macrotermes bellicosus* (below), house up to five million termites and are highly complex buildings, with full air conditioning. Nests usually have a single queen, who lays all the eggs, and a single king, who fertilizes them all. In a really big nest, a queen and king may live for 15 years, and for much of her life the queen will lay one egg every three seconds. She lives in a special chamber, fed constantly by the numerous workers. Radiating out from the nest are many covered trails, guarded by large soldier termites, along which the workers bring all the food needed for the colony.

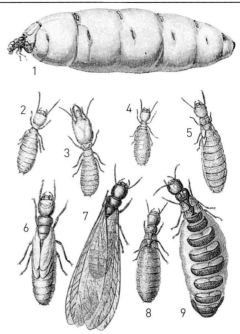

Termite castes
1) *Macrotermes* queen; 2) worker; 3) soldier; 4) young nymph; 5) short-winged nymph; 6) long-winged nymph; 7) male; 8) young female; 9) egg-laying female.

Nest of *Macrotermes bellicosus*

Air-conditioned city

This towering mound is really a ventilation chimney through which hot air from the nest can escape. Beneath the tower is a cave about 9 ft (3 m) in diameter, housing the nursery galleries, the queen's cell, and the fungus gardens that the termites cultivate for food. Water is obtained from deep cavities below the main cave.

Nest of *Cubitermes*

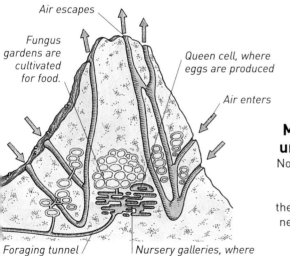

Air escapes

Fungus gardens are cultivated for food.

Queen cell, where eggs are produced

Air enters

Foraging tunnel

Nursery galleries, where larvae are tended

Mysterious umbrellas
No one really knows the function of these umbrella nests of the African *Cubitermes* (right). A nest starts hidden underground. Then, one or more columns may suddenly be built, and up to five caps may be added to each one.

Walls are made from tiny pellets of earth cemented together with saliva

Inside a termites' nest
Air vents at the top of the *Macrotermes subhyalinus* nest (above) allow the termites to control the temperature inside.

Social ants

Most ant species live and work together in big colonies, often building complex nests in which to rear their young. Each nest is begun by a single queen, who lays all the eggs; there is no king. Ant species vary greatly. There are solitary and parasitic species, ants that rear workers from other nests as slaves, and "cuckoo" queens that enter nests and persuade the workers to kill their queen so they can raise her brood.

Anteaters
Anteaters feed on ants, and have powerful claws to break open nests and a long snout to reach inside.

Weight lifters
Ants can lift objects that weigh more than they do. If threatened, the ants' first priority is to carry the brood to safety. The white objects in this photograph (above) are pupae, each with an almost mature adult inside.

Wood ants
In forests, wood ants are important insect predators and a big colony will collect thousands of insects in one day. A large nest may contain 100,000 ants with several queens, and it can last for many years.

The leaves are carried into the nest and used as a basis for growing a kind of fungus, on which the ants feed.

The ants in the nest cut the leaves into smaller pieces and fertilize the fungus gardens with their waste.

The fungus flourishes only if attended to by the ants—if neglected, it will quickly die.

Bits of leaf are left at the entrance of the nest for the gardener ants to pick up and drag inside.

Leaf-cutter ants

A colony of leaf-cutter ants consumes a vast quantity of leaves. These tropical American leaf-cutter ants (*Atta cephalotes*) have cut out pieces of leaves and flowers and are carrying them back to their nest. Here, they are cut up into smaller pieces and used to grow a kind of fungus, on which the ants feed. The nest is usually underground, and has special air conditioning to ensure that the temperature and humidity remain almost constant. A large nest may be several feet across and will house several fungus gardens and separate brood chambers.

Ants returning to collect more leaves

An ant can carry a piece of leaf more than twice its size.

Honeypot ants

In semi-desert areas, ants have found a remarkable way of staying alive in the dry season. In the wet season, the ants feed some of their workers with water and nectar. These workers store the extra food in their abdomens. They cannot move, but hang upside down in the nest as living larders, for use by the rest of the colony.

Weaver ants

Weaver ants build nests in trees by "sewing" together groups of large leaves. A row of worker ants pulls two leaves together. More workers, each holding a live ant larva in their jaws, sew the leaves together using strands of silk produced by the larva's salivary glands. The finished nest (above right) is a ball of leaves.

Ball and socket joint allows movement in all directions

Antenna

Eye

Sense hairs

Toothed jaws for gripping food

Jaws

The shape of an ant's jaws depends on the food it eats. Most ants are predators, with long, pointed jaws. This Asian tree-living ant (above) has simple jaws, with a few teeth for feeding on soft insects and honeydew.

Palps for sensing and manipulating food

These leaf-cutter ants are looking for pieces of leaf to cut out and carry to their nest.

Ant

Two ants cut out a large piece of leaf with their sharp, pointed jaws

A leafy trail

Trails of leaves can often be seen during the day as the ants cross footpaths on the route back to the nest. Outward-bound workers can be seen stopping to encourage their colleagues.

The "parasols" of these leaf-cutter ants are pieces of leaves and flowers.

Fair-weather workers

Leaf-cutter ants do not collect leaves when it is raining, and if a heavy shower occurs while they are out cutting, the leaves are usually dropped outside the nest. Wet leaves may upset the delicate balance inside the fungus gardens and endanger the colony's food supply.

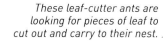

Honeybees and hives

People have collected honey from the nests of bees for many centuries. The oldest record is a cave painting in Spain, nearly 9,000 years old, which shows a figure taking honey from a nest on a cliff. In a modern domestic hive, there are three types of honeybee (*Apis mellifera*): one queen (a fertile female who lays all the eggs); a few hundred males called drones, whose function is to fertilize new queens; and up to 60,000 female workers, who do all the work in the hive.

Busy bees
Straw bee skeps, like this one (above), drawn 400 years ago, changed little for thousands of years.

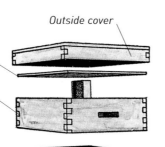

Swarming
A bee colony produces a few new queens each year. Just before the first queen emerges from her pupa, the old queen and about half the workers fly away as a swarm. This engraving shows a swarm being gathered into a straw skep.

Lower frame
On the lower frames of a hive (right), honey and pollen are stored in the upper cells, and the brood is reared in the lower cells. When a bee finds a source of nectar, it flies back to the hive and performs a curious "dance" on the comb. This tells other bees how close the food is.

Large drone cells

Outside cover

Inside cover

Shallow super

Queen excluder—a grid with slots to prevent the queen laying eggs in the upper combs

Modern hives
The modern Langstroth hive was invented in 1851 in the USA. The bees are provided with combs in removable frames—a lower set for the brood chamber and an upper set (shallow super) for storing nectar and pollen.

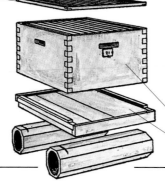

Brood chamber

Bottom board with hive entrance

Cell walls are made of wax, which the workers produce in flakes from glands between the joints of their abdomens

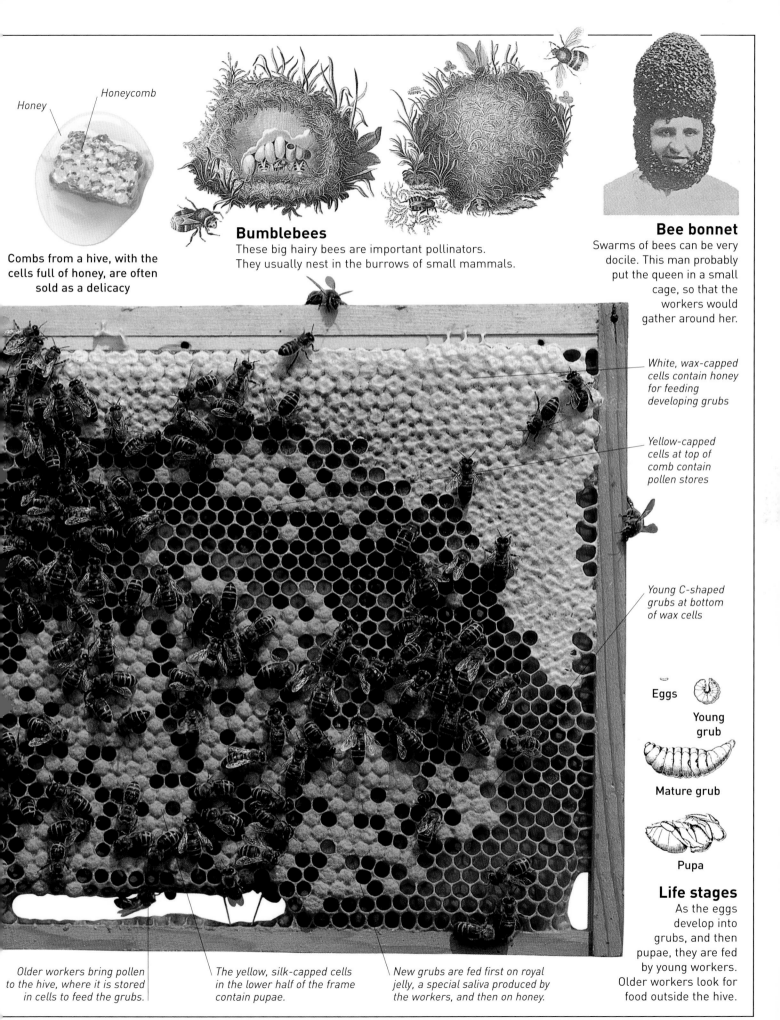

Honey

Honeycomb

Combs from a hive, with the cells full of honey, are often sold as a delicacy

Bumblebees

These big hairy bees are important pollinators. They usually nest in the burrows of small mammals.

Bee bonnet

Swarms of bees can be very docile. This man probably put the queen in a small cage, so that the workers would gather around her.

White, wax-capped cells contain honey for feeding developing grubs

Yellow-capped cells at top of comb contain pollen stores

Young C-shaped grubs at bottom of wax cells

Eggs

Young grub

Mature grub

Pupa

Life stages

As the eggs develop into grubs, and then pupae, they are fed by young workers. Older workers look for food outside the hive.

Older workers bring pollen to the hive, where it is stored in cells to feed the grubs.

The yellow, silk-capped cells in the lower half of the frame contain pupae.

New grubs are fed first on royal jelly, a special saliva produced by the workers, and then on honey.

Helpful and harmful

Insects are essential to our well-being. Bees, flies, and butterflies help pollinate our crops; wasps and ladybugs destroy the caterpillars and aphids that attack our plants; beetles and flies clean up rotting plants; moth caterpillars produce silk; and food coloring is made from the crushed bodies of certain bugs. However, insects can also be a nuisance. Many insects transmit diseases to people, animals, and plants, and every year they are responsible for the destruction of between 10 and 15 percent of the world's food.

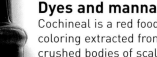
Harvesting cochineal insects

Dyes and manna
Cochineal is a red food coloring extracted from the crushed bodies of scale insects (*Dactylopius coccus*). The biblical manna that fed the children of Israel was probably derived from similar bugs on tamarisk trees.

Cochineal coloring

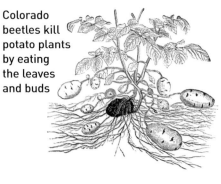
Colorado beetles kill potato plants by eating the leaves and buds

Colorado beetle
When potatoes were introduced to North America in about 1850, the Colorado beetle (*Leptinotarsa decemlineata*, above) swept from potato patch to potato patch, killing vast numbers of plants as it went. In the days before insecticides, it was a serious pest.

Periodic pest
The longhorn beetle (*Hoplocerambyx spinocorrus*, left) usually attacks dead and dying sal trees in India. The grubs drill large tunnels in the timber. But sometimes, the population increases rapidly and living trees are attacked, causing widespread damage.

Silk moth harvest
Silk has been produced for 5,000 years. Silk moth caterpillars are picked from mulberry trees, so that silk can be harvested from their cocoons.

Poison darts
The pupae of this African leaf beetle (*Polyclada bohemani*, above) contain a powerful poison, once used by South African hunters.

Deathwatch beetles can reduce timbers to little more than a skeleton.

Unwelcome guests
In 1920, two visitors to Alexandria, in Egypt, spent a night catching bedbugs rather than sleeping. By morning, they had collected 700 bugs.

Deathwatch beetles
Deathwatch beetles (*Xestobium rufovillosum*) can be serious pests of timber in houses.

Locusts
(*Schistocerca gregaria*)

Nymph

Nymph

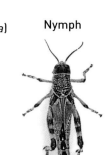

Adult

Adult locusts have wings, but the nymphs are wingless

Devastating locusts

Most of the time, locusts act like solitary grasshoppers. But when they gather in groups, their body structure, color, and behavior change, and they form swarms. The wingless nymphs eat everything on the surrounding ground, while adults fly great distances.

Locusts swarming

If a locust swarm breeds uncontrolled for a few months, the number of individuals can reach thousands of millions. Such a plague will eat all the available plants in an area, leaving the human population destitute.

Home wreckers

Termites will sometimes eat away the wooden structure of a house from within the timbers, leaving just the thin painted surface undamaged. This door lintel (right) was once 28 cm (11 in) square.

Grain weevils

Flour pests

The red-rust flour beetle is a common pest in packages of flour. The larvae of grain weevils live inside the kernels of stored cereals, making them useless for flour production.

Leaf galls on American vine

Red-rust flour beetles

Adult aphid

Adult aphid with wings

Disease spreaders

Mosquitoes are bloodsucking flies with biting mouthparts that inject diseases such as yellow fever and malaria into humans.

Grapevine pest

Viteus vitifoliae (above) became an aphid pest of grapevines that reached Europe from America in 1860. Within 25 years it destroyed 2.5 million acres (1 million hectares) of vines through the galls it produced on the roots.

Spider beetles

Both adults and larvae of these spiderlike beetles (*Ptinus tectus*) feed on dried food, spices, and grain. They are common pests in warehouses.

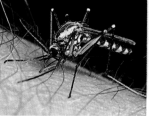

Spider beetles feeding on a dried stock cube

Termites only eat the softer parts of the wood—the hard parts are left.

Looking at insects

In the 19th century, interest in natural history became fashionable, and private collections of insects were common. Today, insect collecting is concerned more with examining the ways in which insects help maintain the balance of nature. But looking at insects can be fun. All it requires is patience and good eyesight—possibly helped by a magnifying glass. Just observing how these fascinating creatures live is an important way of learning about the natural world.

Insect interest
This engraving (above) is of an elaborate glass tank called a vivarium, in which the life cycles of living insects could be observed.

Jean Fabre (1823–1915)
The French naturalist Jean Henri Fabre wrote many popular books about the lives of insects.

Chloroform bottle and top

Carrying ring

Nozzle

Airtight top

Chloroform bottle
Chloroform, kept in containers like this one (left), was once used to kill freshly caught insect specimens.

Ivory-handled pin

Specimen fixed in front of lens for examination

Dustproof leather case

Mounted lens
This mounted lens (right), with its ivory handle, was used for many years by the English collector Edward Meyrick (1854–1938).

Hand lens
Magnifying glasses used by insect collectors often folded up to fit in a pocket.

Folding brass lens

Small high-power lens

Cork

Insects pinned into cork

Collecting tin
Insect collectors pinned their fragile specimens in special cork-lined tins like this one (right).

Field diary
The diaries of the English entomologist Charles Dubois (1656–1740) include notes of the insects he saw, often with drawings and comments on their habits and appearance.

Scissorlike handles

This old-fashioned scissor net (left) was snapped shut to trap an insect

Square tips for holding pins

Fine points for tiny insects

Opticians' forceps

Finely woven cotton muslin prevents the captured insect from escaping.

Metal needle holder

Tweezers

Tools
Opticians' forceps with fine points are useful for picking up tiny specimens. In contrast, tweezers with square tips are used for holding pins.

Old pin box

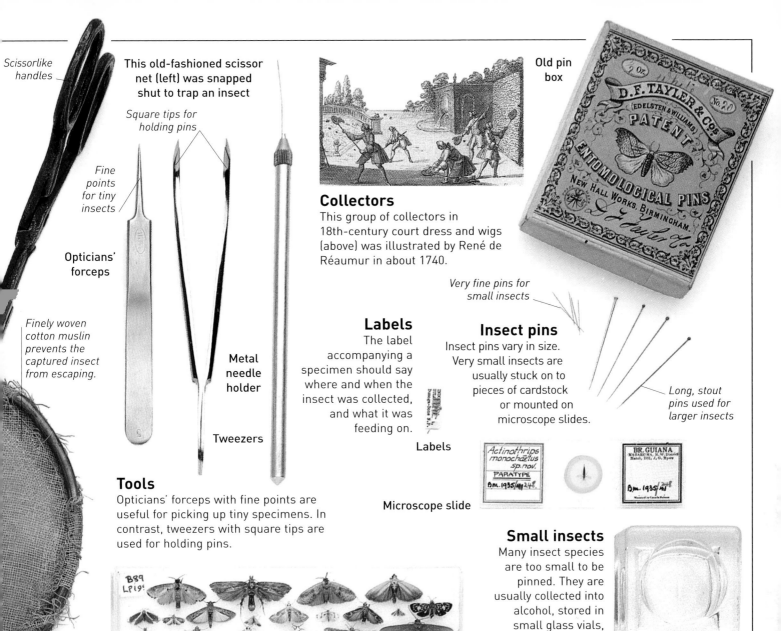

Collectors
This group of collectors in 18th-century court dress and wigs (above) was illustrated by René de Réaumur in about 1740.

Very fine pins for small insects

Labels
The label accompanying a specimen should say where and when the insect was collected, and what it was feeding on.

Insect pins
Insect pins vary in size. Very small insects are usually stuck on to pieces of cardstock or mounted on microscope slides.

Long, stout pins used for larger insects

Labels

Microscope slide

Small insects
Many insect species are too small to be pinned. They are usually collected into alcohol, stored in small glass vials, and studied under a microscope.

Glass dish containing alcohol

Base of box is lined with white plastic foam

Modern plastic collection box
Plastic boxes are lighter than metal ones, and collections can be seen through the lid. Above is a typical collection of small moths.

Modern traps
The Malaise trap catches large numbers of flying insects. When they fly into the central wall, most crawl upward into the bottle at the top.

Extinction
In recent years, radical changes in land use have reduced many areas of natural habitat, resulting in many insect species becoming extinct. Among those now considered extinct is the St. Helena earwig. This very large insect, which used to live only on the island of St. Helena in the South Atlantic Ocean, has not been seen for many years.

Extinct St. Helena earwig

Did you know?

A cockroach can live for up to three months without its head.

The bombardier beetle defends itself by firing boiling hot liquid from its abdomen. The gas is formed by a chemical reaction and irritates the eyes of the enemy, acting as a smokescreen while the beetle scuttles off to safety.

The color of an adult head louse can be determined by the color of the person's hair in which it lives.

The tallest known insect nest is one built by a colony of African termites. It measured 42 ft (12.8 m) high.

One of the most deadly species of insect on Earth is the desert locust, or *Schistocerca gregaria*. The danger lies not in a direct threat posed to humans, but in the havoc wreaked on agriculture when a plague of locusts attacks a crop. The desert locust appears after heavy monsoon rains and devours every single plant in an area, often causing famine among local humans and animals.

A man walks safely through a locust swarm

Killer bees, or Africanized honeybees

A swarm of desert locusts may have up to 40 billion members. It can travel 400 sq miles (1,036 sq km) and eat 44,000 tons of plants a day, enough to feed a city with a population of 400,000 people for a year.

Sorting silkworm cocoons to make silk

Queen termites have been known to lay an egg a second—that adds up to an incredible 30 million eggs a year.

Killer bees, one of the most deadly insects on Earth, are not a naturally occurring species. The bees were first bred in Brazil in 1956 when the African honeybee was crossed with local bees in an attempt to increase their honey yield. However, the new breed turned out to be aggressive, with a tendency to attack both humans and animals.

Hawk moths can fly at speeds of 33.3 mph (53.6 km/h).

The silkworm (*Bombyx mori*) is the caterpillar of a moth whose cocoon is used to make silk. The silk is a single, continuous thread made from protein and secreted by two glands at either side of the caterpillar's head. To harvest, the silkworm is allowed to spin its cocoon and is then placed in boiling water to kill the pupa and help unravel the thread.

Young desert locust

Questions and Answers

Q How many species of insects are there overall?

A There are at least one million different species of insects in total. Insects form around 80 percent of all animal life on Earth and, of this, ants and termites each make up 10 percent. It is estimated that there are one billion insects for every human being.

Q Which insect can withstand the hottest temperatures?

A The adults and the larvae of the *Scatella thermarum* are found in hot springs in Iceland and can live in temperatures as hot as 118°F (48°C), which is too hot for most people to put their hands into.

Q What is the best way to repel insects?

A Natural insect repellents that can be worn on the skin include oil mixtures containing cedar, tea tree, lavender, or vanilla. Some people believe that eating garlic may keep

Garlic can keep insects at bay

insects at bay—especially blood-hungry pests such as mosquitoes. This is because garlic emits an odor when absorbed into the blood, which many insects find unpleasant.

Q What is an insect's favorite food?

A Although many insects have very precise diets, some are not fussy and will eat almost anything, including wood, shoe polish, and paper!

Q Can insects be eaten?

A Many peoples of the world include insects as part of a nutritious diet. One example is the annual moth feast held by the Aboriginal peoples in the Bogong mountains of New South Wales, Australia. Moths are cooked in hot sand. After the heads have been removed, the moths' bodies are ground into a paste and baked as cakes. Other popular insect meals around the world include fried grasshoppers, roasted crickets, and larvae paste.

Q Do insects have brains?

A Yes. An ant brain, for example, has about

250,000 brain cells. A human brain has 10,000 million cells, so a colony of 40,000 ants has collectively the same size brain power as a human being.

Q What is the biggest ant colony ever known?

A A supercolony of *Formica yessensis* on the coast of Japan is reported to have been home to more than one million queens and 306 million worker ants living in 45,000 interlinked nests underground.

Q Which insect has the longest body?

A One species of stick insects, *Pharnacia kirbyi*, has the longest body of all insects. Females can reach up to 14 in (36 cm) long.

Stick insect

Q Which is the loudest insect?

A The African cicada *Brevisana brevis* produces a sound pressure at a level of 106.7 decibels over a distance of 19.5 in (50 cm). This is the loudest insect call on record. Insect songs form a vital part of communication, defense, and reproduction.

Record Breakers

HIGHEST JUMPER
• Proportional to its body size, a tiny flea can jump the highest of any insect, equivalent to a human being jumping 24.6 ft (7.5 m) into the air.

TINIEST INSECT
• The tiny parasite *Megaphragma caribea* from Guadeloupe in the Caribbean is one of the smallest insects known, measuring just 0.006 in (0.017 cm).

FASTEST FLIER
• Dragonflies can speed through the air at up to 35 mph (56 km/h).

MOST WINGBEATS
• In scientific tests, a tiny midge can flap its wings up to 50,000 times per minute, compared with 300 times per minute for the average butterfly.

Ants form 10 percent of all animal life

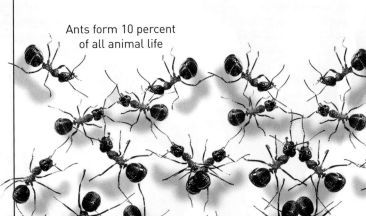

Insect classification

There are more than one million species of known insects in the world. Here are the main insect groups.

Flies, gnats, and mosquitoes

Including around 90,000 species, this group contains the household fly as well as bloodsuckers such as mosquitoes. Flies can transmit diseases by contaminating food with organisms picked up on their legs and mouthparts.

Hoverfly

The hoverfly is often mistaken for a wasp

Flying cockroach

Cockroaches

Cockroaches include around 5,500 different species and have been present on Earth for more than 400 million years. Cockroaches are very sturdy insects and can run at speeds of nearly 1.8 mph (3 km/h).

Drone bumblebee

Bugs

This group includes greenflies, shield bugs, cicadas, and water striders. Shield bugs are often called "stink bugs" because they can produce a horrible smell by emitting a fluid from their glands.

Shield bug

Crab louse

Lice

These wingless parasites infest humans and animals, laying eggs in hair-covered parts of the body and feeding on skin and blood.

Bees and wasps

Although feared for their stings, bees and wasps are key to flower pollination and feed on smaller insects that are harmful to crops. They are social creatures that often live in communities.

Stick insects

Containing around 2,500 species, these insects are mostly found in the tropics. Stick insects may or may not have wings and are often bred as pets.

Stick insect

Stag beetle

Beetles

The largest single group in insect classification, beetles include animals as diverse as the wingless glow worm, the woodworm, and the ladybug.

Ant

Ants

Ants are among the most numerous of the insect species and are thought to comprise 10 percent of all animal life on Earth.

Swallowtail butterfly

Butterflies and moths

Numbering more than 300,000 species in all, this group can be found all over the world.

Eyespots may divert predators away from delicate body

Praying mantises

There are about 1,700 varieties of praying mantis. Most species live in warm climates. The female mantis may eat the male after mating.

Praying mantis

Mantis females are among the largest insects

Stone fly

Stone flies

So-called because they are often seen resting on stones, these aquatic insects number around 2,000 named species. They are a favorite food of fish such as trout.

Flea

Fleas

Feeding off animals, a flea's diet consists of blood. An average flea can consume up to 15 times its own body weight in blood daily. This insect spends 95 percent of its life as an egg, larva, or pupa, and only five percent as an adult. Adult fleas cannot survive without regular blood meals.

Scorpionfly

Scorpionflies

This small group includes only 400 species, most of which measure around 0.8 in (2 cm) in length. They get their name from the male tail, which is turned upward like a scorpion's, although it carries no sting.

Silverfish

Bristletails

The 600 species of bristletails are found worldwide. Silverfish do not have any wings and are often found scavenging for food in domestic households.

Thrips love to feed on flowers.

Thrips

Dragonflies

Dragonflies are so-called because of their fierce jaws, although they actually use their legs to catch prey. These insects were in existence long before the dinosaurs.

Grasshopper

Grasshoppers and crickets

This group contains 17,000 species and also includes the troublesome desert locust. Crickets have long antennae, and many species are called "katydids" in North America.

Thrips

These tiny insects measure just 0.1 in (0.25 cm) in length and number around 3,000 species. They live among crops and can cause real damage to harvests.

Dragonfly

Lacewings feed on other insects.

Lacewings

So called because of their delicate, veined wings, this insect group includes more than 6,000 species. Lacewing larvae hide from their predators under the empty skins of their prey.

Adult mayflies cannot eat and so die quickly.

Mayfly

Mayflies

These beautiful insects can spend up to three years as a nymph and then perish after just a few hours as an adult.

Lacewing

Find out more

To get more insight into the world of creepy crawlies without getting too close and personal, check out your nearest natural history museum. Here you can examine preserved insect specimens kept safely at bay behind glass! However, some of the most fun expeditions can start at home.

Natural history museums
One of the best places to learn about insects is at a natural history museum, such as the American Museum of Natural History (above). Here you can find exhibitions of ancient and modern insects, carefully collected through the years.

A natural history exhibition

USEFUL WEBSITES

- Bug Bios: an illustrated database of very cool bugs **www.insects.org**
- Search for an insect on this comprehensive BBC database **www.bbc.co.uk/nature/wildlife/**
- Website of London's Natural History Museum, with a creepy crawlies gallery and insect webcams **www.nhm.ac.uk/nature-online/life**

Natural history exhibitions
When you visit a natural history museum, there will usually be a section devoted to entomology, or the study of insects. Here you can view preserved specimens of many exotic species from around the globe without ever having to leave your own country!

Stones, wood, and dead leaves often hide busy insect colonies beneath.

Countryside
Upturn any piece of wood and you will find busy colonies working away. In summer, you can also observe insects in search of nectar on clusters of flowers.

Sticky food residue attracts hungry insects.

The fly uses its legs and mouthparts to taste and pick up food.

A household fly

At home

Every home is abundant with insect life, both seen and unseen. In summer, a constant flow of insect traffic can be logged. Flies are often to be found in the kitchen, scavenging for leftover food. Bees, wasps, and all manner of flying insects zoom in through open windows, while moths head toward bright lights at night. Invisible insect life is everywhere, on both animal and human bodies, as well as in furnishings.

PLACES TO VISIT

EDINBURGH BUTTERFLY AND INSECT WORLD, EDINBURGH, SCOTLAND
See exotic butterflies, ugly bugs, and busy ants in this rain forest environment.

NATURAL HISTORY MUSEUM, SOUTH KENSINGTON, LONDON, ENGLAND
The creepy crawly gallery hosts exciting interactive exhibitions and videos.

OXFORD UNIVERSITY MUSEUM OF NATURAL HISTORY, OXFORD, ENGLAND
The entomology collection here is the second largest in the UK, and the reference library contains 15,000 books.

O ORKIN INSECT ZOO, NATURAL HISTORY MUSEUM, WASHINGTON, DC, USA
Observe insects in their natural environment. In here, volunteers demonstrate tarantula feeding, and visitors may hold some of the insects.

AUDUBON NATURE INSTITUTE INSECTARIUM, NEW ORLEANS, LOUISIANA, USA
Child-friendly exhibits explain the life of insects, from butterfly life cycles to what termites are up to.

Note the colors and shapes of the insects you find.

Net gently captures flying insects for inspection

Tiny insects can be seen in detail under a glass.

Notebook for recording information

Butterfly net

Discovery kit

A soft butterfly net allows you to catch flying insects, which can temporarily be placed in a glass jar while you make notes. A garden trowel can be used to dig up soil and view insects underground.

Magnifying glass

Make holes in the lid to allow air to enter the jar and the insects to breathe

Glass jar

Trowel for turning over soil

Glossary

Antenna

Exoskeleton

Red spotted longhorn beetle

ABDOMEN
The rear part of an insect's body.

ANTENNAE
The sensory organs on each side of the head, also called feelers, used for navigation, taste, "sight," and hearing.

ARTHROPOD
An invertebrate with a jointed body case, such as an insect or a spider. Insects and spiders are often confused with each other, but unlike spiders, insects have three separate body parts, three pairs of legs, and antennae.

BENEFICIAL INSECTS
Any insect that has a lifestyle that is beneficial to humans, such as pollinators and recyclers.

CAMOUFLAGE
When an insect adopts the color or texture of its surrounding environment to conceal itself from predators or prey.

CATERPILLAR
The larva of a moth, butterfly, or sawfly.

CERCI
The paired structures that spring from the tip of the abdomen in many insects.

Crow swallowtail caterpillar

CHITIN
The tough material that makes up an insect's exoskeleton.

CHRYSALIS
The pupa of a butterfly or moth.

COCOON
A covering composed either partly or wholly of silk and spun by many larvae as a protection for the pupae.

COLONY
A local population, often produced by a single queen.

COMPOUND EYE
An eye made up of many separate compartments.

ENTOMOLOGY
The study of insects. An entomologist is a scientist who studies insects.

ENVELOPE
A protective covering made by some wasps for their nests. In common wasps, the envelope is constructed from chewed wood fibers and saliva.

EXOSKELETON
The hard outer case that surrounds an insect's body.

GRUB
A thick-bodied larva with thoracic legs (legs attached to the thorax) and a well-developed head.

Centipede, an arthropod but not an insect

HIND
Relating to the back part, such as hind legs or hind wings.

INVERTEBRATE
An animal without a backbone.

LARVA
An immature insect that looks different from its parents, and often eats different food. When a larva is mature, it undergoes complete metamorphosis.

MAGGOT
A larva without legs and without a well-developed head.

MANDIBLES
The first pair of jaws in insects. These are toothlike in chewing insects, pointed in sucking insects, and form the upper jaw of biting insects.

MAXILLA
The second pair of jaws that some insects possess.

METAMORPHOSIS
The series of changes that an insect undergoes between its early life and adulthood. Insects that undergo incomplete metamorphosis change gradually as they grow up. Ones that undergo complete metamorphosis change abruptly, during a resting stage called a pupa.

MOLTING
In insects, the process of shedding the exoskeleton.

MOTTLED
A surface with blotchy color variation or difference.

NECTAR
The sugary liquid secreted by many flowers on which some insects feed.

NYMPH
The name given to the young stages of insects that undergo incomplete metamorphosis. The nymph is usually similar to the adult except that its wings are not fully developed.

OCELLUS
The simple eyes in larvae, which detect light and dark but cannot form images.

OOTHECA
An egg case, such as the purselike structure carried around by cockroaches.

Butterflies undergo metamorphosis

SEGMENT
One of the rings or divisions of the body, or one of the sections of a jointed limb.

SOCIAL
Insects such as ants or bees that live in organized communities of individuals.

SOLDIER
In termites and ants, soldiers protect and guard the colony from intruders and predators.

TARSUS
The foot or jointed appendage at the end of the leg.

TIBIA
The fourth joint of an insect's leg.

THORAX
The second or intermediate part of the body, corresponding roughly to the chest region in humans.

TRACHEAE
Tubes in the body of an insect that transport oxygen around.

TRUE FLIES
Those flies that have only one pair of wings. The remnants of a second pair of wings, known as halteres, function as stabilizers or airspeed detectors during flight.

TYMPANUM
The vibratory membrane in various parts of an insect's body that serves as an eardrum.

ULTRAVIOLET
Beyond the violet end of the light spectrum, ultraviolet is invisible to most mammals, but visible to most insects.

WORKER
A member of an insect colony that is sterile (cannot breed) and whose duties include finding food for the colony.

OVIPOSITOR
The tubular egg-laying apparatus of a female insect.

PALP
A segmented leglike structure. Palps have a sensory function and play a role in tasting food.

PARASITE
An organism that spends part or all of its life in close association with another species, taking food from it but giving nothing in return.

POLLEN
Fertilizing powder or grains produced by a flower and often carried from plant to plant by insects.

PREDATOR
An insect that preys on or hunts another animal to kill it for food.

PROBOSCIS
Any extended mouth structure, usually applied to the mouth of flies, the beak of bugs, and the tongue of butterflies and moths.

PROLEG
An insect larva's abdominal leg, distinguished from a "true" leg.

PUPA
The stage of complete metamorphosis, between larva and adult.

QUEEN CELL
The cell in which a queen honey bee develops from egg to adult.

ROSTRUM
A snout or beaklike feature; usually refers to a piercing mouthpart.

SCAVENGER
An insect that feeds on human waste or on dead plants or animals.

Microscopic view of longhorn beetle

Teeth for gripping prey

Mandibles, or jaws

Antennae are made up of jointed segments

Compound eye can detect the slightest movement

Insects can see ultraviolet light

Index

Acknowledgments

The author would like to thank his many colleagues at the Natural History Museum who helped with this project, particularly Sharon Shute, Judith Marshall, Bill Dolling, George Else, David Carter, Nigel Fergusson, John Chainey, Steve Brooks, Nigel Wyatt, Philip Ackery, Peter Broomfield, Bill Sands, Barry Bolton, Mick Day, and Dick Vane-Wright.

Dorling Kindersley would like to thank:
Julie Harvey at the Natural History Museum, London Zoo, Dave King for special photography on pp.56–57, David Burnie for consultancy, and Kathy Lockley for picture research.

For this edition, the publisher would also like to thank: Dr. George McGavin for consultancy; Claire Bowers, David Ekholm–JAlbum, Sunita Gahir, Jo Little, Nigel Ritchie, Susan St. Louis, Carey Scott, & Bulent Yusuf for the clipart; David Ball, Neville Graham, Rose Horridge, Jo Little, & Sue Nicholson for the wallchart; BCP, Marianne Petrou, & Owen Peyton Jones for checking the digitized files; and Hazel Beynon for editing the relaunch version and Victoria Pyke for proofreading it.

The publisher would like to thank the following for their kind permission to reproduce their images:

Picture credits
b = bottom, c = center, f = far,
l = left, m = middle, r = right, t = top

Aldus Archive: 61bl. Angel, Heather/ Biophotos: 7br; 10m; 11tr. Biophoto Associates: 36ml; 41br. Boorman, J.: 42m. Borrch, B./Frank Lane: 18tl. Borrell, B./ Frank Lane: 56tr; 67cr. Bunn, D.S.: 50tl. Burton, Jane/Bruce Coleman: 31b; 34mr; 36tl; 39br. Cane, W./Natural Science Photos: 32m; 61bm. Clarke, Dave: 23tm; 47b. Clyne, Densey/Oxford Scientific Films: 57tl; 57tm;
57tr. Cooke, J.A.L./Oxford Scientific Films: 12tl. Corbis: Benjamin Lowy 68bl. Couch, Carolyn/ Natural History Museum: 15br. Craven, Philip/ Robert Harding Picture Library: 7t. Dalton, Stephen/NHPA: 37ml. David, Jules/Fine Art Photos: 38tr. Courtesy of FAAM: BAE Systems Regional Aircraft 12–13ca; With thanks to Maureen Smith and the Met Office UK. Photo by Doug Anderson 13cr. Fogden, Michael/ Oxford Scientific Films: 10ml. Foto Natura Stock/FLPA: 66cr. Goodman, Jeff/NHPA: 9ml. Hellio & Van Ingen/NHPA: 64bl. Holford, Michael: 15mr. Hoskings, E. & D.: 39tm. James, E.A./NHPA: 46br. King, Ken/Planet Earth: 57m. Kobal Collection: 40tl. Krist, Bob/Corbis: 68cr. Krasemann, S./NHPA: 47tr. Lofthouse, Barbara/ Natural History Museum: 12tr, 14bl, 65tr, 66c. Oliver, Stephen: 69bc. Overcash, David/Bruce Coleman: 15bl. Oxford Scientific Films: 20tl. Packwood, Richard/ Oxford Scientific Films: 56tr. Pitkin, Brian/ Natural History Museum: 42m. Polking, Fritz/FLPA: 64tl. Popperphoto
61tl. Robert Harding Picture Library: 30tl. Rutherford, Gary/Bruce Coleman: 7bm. Sands, Bill: 55m. Shaw, John/Bruce Coleman Ltd: 67br. Shay, A./Oxford Scientific Films: 20bm. Springate, N.D./Natural History Museum: 63bm. Taylor, Kim/Bruce Coleman: 21tl; 31b. Taylor, Kim: 33m. Thomas, M.J./ FLPA: 68b. Vane-Wright, Dick/Natural History Museum: 16br. Ward, P.H. & S.L./Natural Science Photos: 44mr. Williams, C./Natural Science Photos: 36ml. Young, Jerry: 66bl.

Illustrations: John Woodcock: 10, 41, 55; Nick Hall: 13,15

All other images © Dorling Kindersley.

For further information, see:
www.dkimages.com

Evans Picture Library: 61tm, 64tr. Minden Pictures/ FLPA: 71b. National Film Archive: 32tl. Natural History Museum: 12tr, 14bl, 65tr, 66c.

Mary Evans Picture Library: 61tm, 64tr. Minden Pictures/ FLPA: 71b. National Film Archive: 32tl.

Harding Picture Library: 37br. Mary